INTEGRITY
When No One's Looking

THE **NAIL** OF **INTEGRITY**™

MARVIN SOSKIL

PAGE PUBLISHING, INC.
New York, NY

First originally published by Page Publishing, Inc. 2017

ISBN 978-1-68409-902-3 (Paperback)
ISBN 978-1-68409-903-0 (Digital)

Printed in the United States of America

To My Dear Son Brett:
You have always been a caretaker of others and a pillar of strength,
assisting me during my difficult times. You have shown great
courage and tenacity in overcoming a serious personal issue.
In the words of Dan Milman from his book The Way of
the Peaceful Warrior, "When you become a warrior, you
learn to master anything." Being by your side and watching
you fight to get where you need to be, enables us both
to master anything. Through you, I see the light.
I love you, Dad

To Aaron Joshua Soskil, my son who passed away at two and a half
years of age:
His short life made such a tremendous impact on me
that I became so involved in children's charities in his namesake.
"You smile made us smile,
Your innocence made us humble,
Your countenance gave us strength."

and

To Daniel (Danny) Klein, my cousin's son, who was afflicted
with Asperger's syndrome, was the sweetest, kindest, and
most innocent of young men who, at the age of twenty,
decided that this world was too cruel for him to continue
and went to join God, so he could be at peace.

We all have freedom of choice.

Nobody is telling you what you must do.

It's your conscience

that you have to live with!

Contents

Acknowledgements

I have a number of people I would like to thank for their assistance and support in making this book possible. Merely by unforeseen opportunity, the idea of writing this book became inspired through my desire to be creative with a product that I thought to be an inspirational tool at the time. The story is about a metaphysical journey, which I took as a result of the coaching sessions of Pete Cracovaner, president of the Pinnacle Resource Group. Pete showed me how my journey, which stemmed from a dream or desire to reach a destination of greatness, has more to do with enjoying the journey and the reality that ordinary people can do great things. My mastermind group, Jeff Stern, Bruce Zutler, Jerry Allocca, Joseph Scarpa, William Corbett Jr., Robert Kothe, and all of the other colleagues who were instrumental in offering support, mentoring, and assistance along with valuable input and creativity and positive feedback. Thank you to Page Publishing, Inc. for working diligently with me to edit this book, so it makes some sort of sense. Janise, my wife, has been by my side sometimes with reluctance but has always been there to give me support and enabled me to dream. My Mother who at 93 years of age is still an inspiration, who has taught me countenance. My Dad, a World War II hero, who wrote his memoirs at age 90, set a great example for me to follow. I am grateful to all of those who shared this journey with me and to all of you who have become inspired by my thoughts and might embark on such a journey to make a difference.

Several people have impacted me, and I would like to thank you all for your support, believing in me and my projects and giving me the strength shoot for the stars, so I may either accomplish or live my dreams, discover my purpose, and offer my service at the same time. I thank my wife Janise, whose endless support has given me the opportunity to feel that I can accomplish anything that I put my mind to. Her love and compassion has allowed me to follow my dreams. Her moral support has given me countenance; her guidance has kept me in the mode. I can't tell you how many countless times Janise said, "If you come up with another one of your crazy ideas, we're done." And yet, every time I came up with a new idea or chased my dreams, Janise has stood by my side and given me total support. She has been my soundboard, my strongest adversary. I am blessed to have a wife that can put up with me and my antics. I thank my children, who I believe possess great integrity in all that they represent and do. My son Brett has been my right arm. He has always shown me that he was proud of my accomplishments, which has made me feel that I affected his life for the better. His love, his technological support, his expertise in web design, and his support acting as my "personal assistant" have enabled me to keep forging ahead. I am proud of the independent professional that he has become. Thank you to my daughter Jessica, next to my wife, my best friend, whose love and support is constant, and she has dedicated her integrity in the field of Architecture. Thank you to my son Michael, who too has always made me proud. As a father and husband, he has dedicated himself to spending quality time with his family. He and his wife Lori have given their children incredible opportunities to expand their minds through travel, technology, and experiences. Michael received the 2014 Presidential Award for Excellence in Teaching Mathematics at the White House and received the award from President Obama. Michael is totally dedicated to his children and his students so they might learn and gather positive experiences in the learning process, rather than just attend school. Although he passed the principal exam and state certifications to become a principal, he chose to make a greater impact on students as director of technology for the school district, teaching other teachers how to introduce technology in their classrooms. He is constantly contracted by Skype and Microsoft to speak at conferences regarding global collaboration in the classroom for the betterment of students around the world. He has also applied for Global Teacher of the Year, and to date has been nominated in the top fifty out of eight hundred thousand teachers. Michael always shows the greatest level of commitment and integrity than most anyone I know.

Preface

*To thine own self be true, and it must follow, as the night
the day, thou canst not then be false to any man.*
William Shakespeare

* * *

Was there ever something that occurred in your life that became an unforgettable, life changing moment? For me, it was when I stepped on a nail.

Perhaps it was a coincidence or perhaps it a divine intervention, but for whatever reason it became my passion and obsession to send a message to the world.

The following is my story about recognizing what my purpose in life has become.

What pisses you off? Let me ask you this, are there little things that other people do that irritate you? Then, there are those little things along with major things that compelled me to write this book.

Merits and demerits, what do we get in return for the things we do in life? How are we measured for our good deeds? What if we are given demerits for our bad deeds and punished for the thoughtlessness or conscious actions we took by not considering other people's feelings or space? Will you go to heaven or will you go to hell? Who knows? So what are you doing when no one is looking?

I have filled this book with many quotes and excerpts from the notes of scholars and many authors of books, periodicals, and articles, hoping that I may enrich you with insights, which I hope you digest and pass forward. I have written not just for the reader, but for everyone who sees a need to work toward change in the world by your actions and by getting others to think about their actions too. It was through an epiphany that I was inspired to write about integrity and the realization that we should take notice of better ways to serve our communities and the world in which we live. The motivation for writing this book came as a by-product of a project that had nothing to do with writing a book – After all, I'm not a writer, just someone who stepped on a nail.

There was a time that I remember where a handshake meant your word. You made a promise, and you kept it. You agreed to do something, and you did it. Today, it seems as though everything is hit or miss. People say things and make promises with no intention of keeping their word. When you make promises and don't keep them, you lose trust, respect, and credibility with your family, friends, associates, your clients, and others. There are a few special things that could make a difference to me, in my life. If I could get you, the reader, to be more consciousness of your thoughts and actions so that you might strive to be a better person, is the first. If you would make a conscious effort do things a little bit better and to think about your action's and get others to do the same, would be another. If you make a promise, you should make every attempt to keep it. If you take on a project, you should fulfill the obligation to complete it to the best of your ability. If we could adjust people's thought patterns enough, so they have greater integrity, we can all make a difference in the world. How are we going to play with each other? Who is going to make the rules for the games we play, and who is going to keep them?

You must take personal responsibility for your life.
You cannot change the circumstances, the seasons,
or the wind, but you can change yourself.
Jim Rohn

* * *

Taking responsibility for your behavior, your expenditures,
and your actions and not forever supposing that
society must forgive you because it's "not your fault"
is the quality most needed in the next century.
Barbara Tuchman

* * *

It is not what we eat, but what we digest that makes us strong;
not what we gain, but what we save that makes us rich; not what
we read but what we remember…that makes us learned; and not
what we profess…but what we practice that gives us integrity.
Francis Bacon

Introduction

My resolution is to maintain a treasured awareness into everything I do and a greater consciousness of what it is to have integrity. There are many times that I become angry or less tolerant of the actions of other people due to their lack of caring or naïve nature of not knowing that something they did was not congruous with society's rules. When I go the extra mile to perform or correct something I know I did wrong, (something which was not right or could have been done better) I feel a greater sense of calmness and understanding and I feel a desire to reach out and touch others so I can make a more positive impact on the world. We need to alert ourselves toward teaching our children what is right and what is wrong, and how to make this a more congenial place for all of us and all generations moving forward. In our dealings in business, in marriage, in our convictions to our religious beliefs, and in our sense of community and those around us that need a little kindness, we should all strive to be more enriched.

* * *

You're either living in the problem or you're living in the solution. So start living in the solution.
Bob Proctor

* * *

Story:

A farmer, who each day for five years, took his pick and chopped away at a bolder that was blocking part of the path to his farmhouse. Each day he hammered away trying to crack that bolder, but to no avail, his attempts were in vain; however, he had a belief that one day the rock would crumble.

One day, he took that pick and struck that huge boulder, and it split in half as though from the core of the stone. There was a cerebral breach of integrity which split that rock in two.

The moral of the story:

If we maintain unwavering faith in what we believe is so, it will occur. If we make the efforts to create change, in time we will.

Nothing will go for naught.

Do You Believe in a Higher Power?

"One of the most important things on any spiritual journey is our environment. You could have the most amazing seed that will create the strongest tree in the world, but if it's planted in a poor soil and an unsupportive climate, it's not going to become its full potential. In the same sense, you could be doing spiritual work every second of the day and working to transform yourself, but if your environment is not supportive you will not create change, and drastic change is what we need." From an interview with Yehuda Berg, Founder of the Kaballah Center

* * *

As we look around us these days, do you notice how the world has changed? We went from better to worse, worse to horrific and we're heading from horrific to dread?

As I see it, these days, we have instant accessibility to almost any information we seek. Everyone has a smartphone, not just a cell phone; we can travel to far-away places in shorter periods of time; we have the ability to employ financial opportunities at a moment's notice, such as the ability to transfer bank balances, make payments online and other banking transactions; and we can obtain goods and services that people could not have conceived of twenty years ago from our palms. We no longer need to shop in a physical store because now we have the ability to shop online, pay online, and receive packages overnight. We are living longer; we have more access due to the advances in today's technology which has given us opportunities which outdate the once futuristic movie of 1969, 2001 A Space Odyssey. Who could have even imagined that some of these things would come to fruition?

Having the know-how in today's age is like a double-edged sword. We have become inundated with technological advancements, but we also face identity theft, cyber-theft, and cyber-squatting which is making us more vulnerable. Our bank accounts are in jeopardy; our private information becomes available in the cloud for people around the world to gain access to. Sometimes the things that seem to make life easier can also be dangerous if not handled properly.

Technology has grown exponentially and has improved communication media to the point where everything happens in the flash of an eye. The advancements in technology are occurring so rapidly. It's so amazing that when we examine the achievements of the past twenty years dwarfed by the advancements of the past ten years, and the advancements of the past five years dwarfed by those of the last two years, and those of the last two years dwarfed by what happened two weeks ago. Products, programs, procedures, games, and concepts introduced last year are now obsolete by the advancements of today. If you don't keep up with technology today, you will get thrown to the lions. There is no choice anymore.

The converse is also true. All of the advances that we have at our fingertips are also leading to our demise. As we depend more on technology, it seems the less we depend on each other.

Software companies like Microsoft, Oracle, Symantec, VMWare, IBM, EMC or HP and companies like SONY, Apple, and Dell have created a built-in obsolescence. When these companies bring new products to market, they have already developed new software, new products, and other programs or devices which will make today's brand new products an anomaly passé before they launch. It is an intentional built-in obsolescence. Although these advancements in technology make life easier, it is constantly changing for the most part, for the better, it seems that we have been losing what should be most important—integrity and respect in the newer generations.

Today there is instant messaging, Instagram, the sharing of photos and other instantaneous information resources, perhaps there is too much instant gratification. As this technology boom has driven us to new heights, the youth of today has become semi-oblivious to the personal touch and personal communication. With the fastest thumbs ever, should we add a new category in the Olympics for gold medal texting? One of the real issues is that with this lack of need for personal contact, don't we also lose the means to communicate face to face?

The younger generation, Millennials and Generation X, has now turned to texting instead of talking. Instead of fifteen texts that say hi, hello, what's up, where R U, our communications have been reduced to acronyms of BTW, OMG, HRU. Conversations that one may have with a simple phone call in two minutes gets dragged out to fifteen minutes of texting and waiting for responses. Our youths can be having five or more conversations with other people at the same time. Unfortunately, this has become the case, and the even worse scenario is that most of us are becoming guilty of the same thing.

As face-to-face communications is lost, and eye-to-eye contact is lost, integrity is doomed.

Interesting fact: A new statistic announced that 73 percent of pedestrian accidents occur because people are texting and not paying attention to what is happening around them. They are texting while crossing streets and bumping into other people because they are not paying attention to the world around them. An article in USA Today, 2013, stated, "The age group most at risk for cell-phone related injuries while walking is adults under 30, and chiefly those between the ages of sixteen and twenty-five, whose injuries ranged from falling off walkways or bridges to walking in front of moving traffic."

Dichotomy of a Nail

Just as the nail can hold a house together and offer strength and stability or it can puncture a tire. Where a new nail offers a sense of protection, a rusty nail can cause tetanus. A nail can be shot from a gun much faster than a person with a hammer can drive it through a piece of wood, just as a reputation can be destroyed in the flash of a fleeting lie.
Robert Kothe, Faxtback

* * *

We're heading for disaster. Here in New York, two police officers were ambushed, shot, and killed by a nineteen-time felon. The public is protesting against the police; the police are protesting against the mayor. Protesters are attacking the police, and the police are fearful of reacting too harshly as they protect themselves in fear of being accused of brutality. When our police officers are under attack, where do we turn for protection?

Tragedy after tragedy; shooting after shooting; stabbing after stabbing; young children being slaughtered; tribes arising, claiming political independence; kidnapping of school girls in Kenya; when will this cease? ISIS has arisen to take over the non-Islamic world with beheadings, torture, and mass killing. Outbreaks of Ebola, which has been around since 1971, has taken the lives of thousands and appears to be unstoppable in a world of modern medicine.

What is happening to our world?

The city of Boston was held hostage when two young men set off two bombs at the Boston Marathon, killing several and badly wounding many others. In New York City, a man pushed another man onto the tracks in front of a moving subway train because he was angry, and this has occurred a few times more since. In Webster, New York, an ex-convict got hold of two high-powered rifles. He set fire to his sister's house. After killing her, he called the volunteer firefighters and reported the fire. When they appeared, he opened fire and shot four of them, killing two and then killed himself. The very next day, a woman pushed a person of Hindu descent in front of an oncoming train in the New York City subway because she hated turban heads. She thought it was a funny sight to watch as another report came about a gunman who entered a New Jersey police station and opened fire and shooting three officers. There are drive-by shootings. Innocent people and more and more innocent children are getting shot.

In Ferguson, Missouri, the fatal shooting of the unarmed teenager, by police, in the summer of 2014 has earned the police severe looks from critics of the way police and the US criminal justice system treat African Americans and other minority groups. This incident led to months of sometimes violent protests in Ferguson and major cities around the country. In the meantime, this incident and another, six months later, when the officer that shot Michael Brown was acquitted and released from the police force with no benefits had stirred up riots. Hard-working innocent people's businesses were burnt to the ground as well as countless physical injuries, arrests, and deaths which occurred as a result of unorganized protesting. Was anything proven by these unruly riots?

A co-pilot locked the captain out of the cockpit and steered a German airline plane with 150 innocent passengers into a mountainside. Everyone died.

We hear about more and more shootings occurring each and every day.

Our politicians are constantly fighing over gun control. Whether this is just a political statement prior to elections, is another story.

All of this has got to stop!

We can have the power to control situations only if we raise the levels of people's consciousness and get back to basics. That's what I would like this book to accomplish.

All of these senseless tragedies, the cost precious lives frighten our neighbors and scare our children. Each day, we hear of more and more of these events arising somewhere in neighborhoods, in schools, in our country, in our world. It seems that our society is crashing down around us. We are losing control of our environment, and we need something greater than ourselves to remind us of our purpose in life. We need an avenue that can bring us back to the morals and levels of respect that is necessary so that we may live in the world together in harmony. Is it that the media is picking up on more of these incidents for the sensationalism of selling advertising time (discussed in a later chapter) or are these things running wild?

It appears that these days, fear motivates our society. People seem to thrive on following tragedy after tragedy, holding on to every moment so that they can have enough informative gossip to converse with friends and neighbors. Today, we do what's easy instead of what is right. Our legal system is being swayed by public opinion, and public opinion is being swayed by the media. Have we gotten further away from what is right and wrong, so that we might be interesting by carrying on with the hottest topics of the day? Reality shows have become the most popular TV shows. The subject matter is usually quite revolting. Is that the real reality of today?

It is the media that is grasping onto sensationalism and scaring the heck out of each one of us. They concentrate on the bad and not on the good. How many times do you turn on the news to see what great things are happening in the world today? Since the incident in Ferguson, the media stopped talking about the Ebola crisis like it never happened. Media is profiting financially on the sensationalism of the day.

Although many people are taught to act in a certain manner, their behavior has been taught to them by the environment where they grew up. Peer pressure and the desire to be bigger and better and to have more than the next guy is testing people's integrity. There is a very fine line if you possess the qualities that allow you to say no, compared to those whose opinions influence you, to defy your true morals and beliefs.

Are we doing what we believe is right?

An article by Paul L. Walker Integrity—Reality or Illusion?

> We switch on our favorite nightly news program, and the announcer lambastes the immoral acts of a well-known evangelist. Christians reel in shock while unbelievers scoff. And we wonder, "What has happened to integrity?"
>
> The headlines in the morning newspaper scream, "Elected leader succumbs to greed and graft." A nation shrugs and the malfeasance is soon forgotten. And we wonder, "What has happened to integrity?"
>
> At a prayer breakfast, a friend confesses to an adulterous affair. Hearts shatter, and families suffer irreparable damage. And we wonder, "What has happened to integrity?"
>
> Integrity—is it reality or illusion?
>
> In America today, morality based on religious truth has all but disappeared. Instead, we rely on our feelings to do what is right in our own eyes. For many, integrity is an illusion.

A new study, led by orthopedic surgeon Dr. Kenneth K. Hansraj finds that use of the cell phone and tablet, with the neck in a bent position, may cause degenerative changes in the spine. An ordinary adult head weighs ten to twelve pounds, but when it's bent at a sixty-degree angle, the forces endured by the neck surge to sixty pounds, says the study. And the cumulative effect of years of that stress can lead to degeneration of the spine itself. Perhaps we should be spending more time being conscious of the world around us instead of being connected to technology all the time. Now with the new Apple Smartwatch, people have become even more connected than ever before.

My wife and I frequently go to the movies. We always get there early, so of course, we watch all the previews. I am pretty much a today type of guy; however, I was mortified to watch how much violence prevails in everyday life. Every single preview, whether for the coming movies or new television shows, had such horrifying and extreme violence. Video games that were for sale are all about killing, taking hostages, destroying the world.

On December 2012, we learned of the Sandy Hook massacre, a prelude to several more of these events, in an elementary school where twenty young children and seven teachers were killed. Recently, four firefighters, who serve to protect, were randomly shot as they were putting out a fire in Webster, New York. Our society is in turmoil.

People are posting on Facebook pages today all about ISIS, how President Obama sucks, gun control in shopping malls, politics, healthcare reforms, Ebola, and shootings. People are texting who they went to lunch with or when they went to the bathroom last, who is advocating having assault weapons for protection, and who wants tight control of all firearms. There are those that are trying to sway the opinions of others, and there are those who post information just to be seen. As we approach a Presidential Election, the candidates are bashing each other rather than discussing issues. It seems as though there are battles to be fought on all grounds. So I ask you, quoting from the book Animal Farm, "Where do I go, George?"

Where are we heading?

A short while ago, there was a situation where a police officer shot an unarmed by an African American teen. There was no indictment to commit the officer. Protesting and riots broke out all around the country, where neighboring businesses and property was damaged and destroyed, and many people were injured. Where did the violence lead us? Shortly after, protesters across the nation swarmed city streets to voice outrage and their demands for police and judicial reform in the wake of Eric Garner's death and the refusal by a grand jury to indict the officer who put a chokehold on him. Where are we heading? This society is heading for a major correction, and it has to start with you and me taking baby steps until we reach strides.

Prior to the 2015 Super Bowl XLIX, it was discovered that the New England Patriots had been deflating the football which gave them an unfair advantage in prior games. Even in sports? BTW, they won the Super Bowl in the last sixteen seconds of the game.

Come on, guys. What gives? This is supposed to be about professional sports.

Integrity is about not having to stop and think
about what you want to do
but
having the clarity to do what you think is right.
Marvin Soskil

What Is Integrity?

The most influential tool we have in your entire arsenal is your integrity. Zig Zigler

If we always strive to do the right thing and if we tell the truth, if we are honest with others, do we have integrity?

Integrity is a combination of all these things and more. It requires consistency. It is something that you must have embedded deep in your soul. You can't just have it some of the time. Anything worth having in life is never easy, just as integrity is something you have to own, not just accomplish. Building integrity requires commitment and consistency.

I'm sure we have all gotten to the point where we wanted to give up on something important because it was just too hard.

Integrity includes knowing the difference between right and wrong, good and bad, acceptable and not acceptable, avoidable and not avoidable.

Even if we possess the highest ideals and best intentions, we don't always know the right thing to say or do. Living with integrity is never easy. We all try the best we can. But every one of us faces dilemmas day in and day out that challenge our sense of right and wrong.

We assume that a person with integrity would not steal, but approximately as much 99 percent of people would not steal as well. However, how many people can say that they truly would not, in a hypothetical case when there are no consequences and many benefits to gain?

Story:

A starving child who knows not to steal is passing a house. She smells the aroma of a freshly cooked loaf of bread. As she catches a glimpse of it cooling on a window sill, she stops to think. No one will see me take it. Would it be wrong for them to take the bread?

There is a difference between someone who would not steal because they do not think it is right and someone who would not steal because they might get caught. There is a difference when someone is in dire need vs. stealing out of greed. Where do we draw the line? How can we justify one and not the other?

From a website "ElegantWoman.Org" Author Eunice "A Woman with Integrity" writes

"Your possessions, the things you acquire or the situation that you may be in has not much to do with who you are. Your character does influence the outcome of your life, but in many ways, it is sometimes externally influenced without the circumstances being ruled by choices and chance.

Your house or your success does not equate to you. Your lack of success or the size of your bank account does not define you.

No matter how many possessions you own does show whether you are a person with integrity. The way you choose to behave, the way you value others, the kind of decisions you make say a lot about you.

Only a person with integrity has the ability to command long-time respect and admiration from young or old, rich or poor. It doesn't matter what you have now; you can live with integrity and elegance. And you can take the utmost pride in that. That is because integrity is something you decide to have. It is a principle you chose to live by."

*Each of us will someday be judged by our standard
of life, not by the standard of living; by our measure
of giving, not by our measure of wealth; by our
simple goodness, not by seeming greatness.*
William Arthur Ward

* * *

*Dr. Henry Cloud says, "Integrity...the courage to meet
the demand of reality."Character includes more than
ethics and moral. It is everything, depending on what
demands are going to be put upon the design. There
are realities that put demands on people that they have
to meet in order to perform and not to crash.*

* * *

*Character gets you out of bed; commitment
moves you to action. Faith, hope and discipline
enable you to follow through completion.*
Zig Zigler, Over the Top.

The Definition of Integrity

The dictionary defines integrity

as in·teg·ri·ty [in-teg-ri-tee]

1. adherence to moral and ethical principles; soundness of moral character; honesty.
2. the state of being whole, entire, or undiminished.
3. a sound, unimpaired, or perfect condition: the integrity of a ship's hull.
4. the quality of being honest and having strong moral principles; moral uprightness.

"He is known to be a man of integrity."

Integrity can be summed up simply as doing the right thing for the right reason even when no one is watching.

Where honesty is all about telling the truth (which is a moral responsibility), character is who you are versus the reputation of what others think of you. Integrity encompasses both honesty and character and would not be complete without each of them collectively.

There's yet another factor essential to success, and that's character. Vince Gill says, *"Success is always temporary. When all is said and done, the only thing you have left is your character."*

When we combine attitude plus skill and build it on a solid character base, we maximize our ability.

Integrity matters. It encompasses universal values that in themselves promote value and needs of the society in which we live. It sustains the environment, promotes social welfare, and upholds the rights of people.

Integrity Is Destiny

The soul is dyed the color of its thoughts. Think only on those things that are in line with your principles and can bear the light of day. The content of your character is your choice. Day by day, what you choose, what you think, and what you do is who you become. Your integrity is your destiny…it is the light that guides your way.
Heraclitus (535–475 BC)

The one strength we have is the ability to chose integrity over dishonesty. Can you wake up and look in the mirror and be happy with what you see? When I sold my retail jewelry store to 2 brothers, back in 1996, they asked me if I wanted to be partners with them. They suggested that I transfer all of my assets to my wife. Somehow, that sent up a red flag which made me decide to work for them for a salary instead. I made a good decision. They turned out to be less than honest. If I would have become partners with them, I would never be able to look in the mirror and face myself each day. A second blessing was how my parents and Grandparents instilled the importance of our family and the ability to be deeply devoted to the ones you love. A third factor that makes us special, are the people you are hanging out with. Who do you associate with and who do they associate with? If we have been betrayed or violated against by the very people that we associated with, and have wronged others, do we have the ability to return to a life of integrity? Many people have lived a life of indiscretion, of dishonesty, of crime. Even if it is ingrained that a little white lie is okay. That infidelity in marriage can be justified, that cheating on your taxes is a common occurrence because everybody does it, or that driving under the influence is okay, at what point can we claim to be able to live a life of integrity?

Does integrity give us the right to confront those people that we leave doing to wrong thing?

Be Who You Are and Be True to Your Core Beliefs

*The most important opinion you have is the one
of yourself, and the most significant things you
say all day are those you say to yourself.*
Anonymous

* * *

*It's not what you know or who you know—
it's what you are that finally counts.*
Anonymous

* * *

*Operating from the center of one's being and for good character
to happen, you have to be in touch with your inner self, not
being someone else. People of good character have to be able to
stand up to the pressures and say "That is not me"; as a result,
they are internally defined and clear. Too many people stay in
their comfort zones and never step out and try something new.*
Dr. Henry Cloud

* * *

23

There is a saying by Frederick B. Wilcox "If you keep your foot on first base, you'll never get to second." If you don't create positive motion, you will always stay where you are. Nobody can tell you what you should do, what you are allowed to feel or how you should act.

Dr. Henry Cloud, in his book *Integrity: The Courage to Meet the Demands of Reality*, goes on to say that the concept of integrity is about needing wholeness of character. If we do not have integrity of character, the wholeness of character functioning in the ways that we will describe it, then our ability to capitalize on our strengths will be affected.

Sometimes people will fight for something that they believe is right even when perhaps they might be wrong. They become so filled with emotion that they overlook what is real.

Wherever it is in your life you feel that you are absolutely right and somebody else is absolutely wrong, take a step back and see if there is a way both of you are correct, or at the very least, find a way to be tolerant of the other person's point of view. There are usually three sides to every story, so I am told.

When we are so sure we see we see something clearly, that's often the time when we are most blind. Here's a thought that I would like to share.

If you could finish this sentence, The human being is the only animal that? …. What would it say? Think about it for a moment before you read further. In the book *Stumbling on Happiness*, Daniel Gilbert states that the human being is the only animal that thinks about the future. As human beings, we dream, we project, and we are responsible for our own actions.

He writes,

> "Every move that we make is followed by a consequence. If we model our lives with integrity and consider the consequences of our actions, ultimately through little steps, we can change the world and make it a better place."

> As Gilbert considers in his foreword, "An optical illusion is not interesting simply because it causes everyone to make a mistake; rather, it is interesting because it causes everyone to make the same mistake. The errors that optical illusions induce in our perceptions are lawful, regular, and systematic. They are not dumb mistakes but smart mistakes, mistakes that allow those who understand them to glimpse the elegant design and inner workings of the visual system.

> The mistakes we make when we try to imagine our personal futures are also lawful, regular and systematic. They too have a pattern that tells us about the powers and limits of the foresight in much the same way that the optical illusions tell us about the powers and limits of eyesight."

As individuals, we don't think about our actions when we don't consider the consequences of our actions (whether conscious or unconscious), when we accept things on the surface and don't look at people, objects, and responsibilities with integrity, we often lose sight of purpose of life, of the responsibility we each have to our families, our community, and our society today and in the future. We ignore the rights of others and the simple rules that drive society. Perhaps both fear and guilt will cause you to do the right thing in the right way because you are the right kind of person. By doing the right thing with burdens of guilt and fear removed, you feel good about yourself.

Robert Cialdini, in his book Influence Science and Practice, writes that we take much for granted. "We assume life will go on as we know it. We accept mediocrity as a rule because it is easier to live that way. Having integrity is also about giving people a reputation to uphold."

* * *

In an article "How to Build Character through Integrity," Krystle C., Imperatrix and Manuel Montenegro writes,

> "The wonderful thing about character and integrity, which are intimately related, is that they're one of the few things in life that no one will ever be able to forcefully take away from you. Your choices are your own. Even if someone can take your life, they can't force you to make a choice that you believe is wrong."

Grace

The ideal man bears the accidents of life with dignity and grace, making the best of circumstances. Aristotle

* * * *

Happiness cannot be traveled to, owned, earned, worn or consumed. Happiness is the spiritual experience of living every minute with love, grace, and gratitude.
Denis Waitley

* * * *

Another term that encompasses integrity is the idea of grace. Grace can be defined as an extended favor to others, not because they have earned it in some way, but because we just possess it to give. Favor is furthermore defined as a blessing, goodness, integrity. Some people say it is to have unmerited favor. This occurs because people of grace always leave others better off than they were when they were getting nothing in return. This kind of person maintains the standard and forces other people to meet the standard by just being their own being.

Integrity, the kind that meets the demand of reality, is a character that can handle another person's not being all that he/she can be.

In Influence Science and Practice, Robert Cialdini also speaks of how reciprocation equals power:

As in the case of a gift, or when you offer something to someone, or do them a favor, is there an obligation for them to do something in return? We greatly increase the chance that we will do what they wish, merely by providing us with a small favor prior to their request. The rule possesses awesome strength, often producing a yes response to a request that except for an existing feeling of indebtedness, would have surely been refused. It normally affects the decision to comply. With this in mind, when you make a suggestion to someone to do something better, which benefits them and perhaps the society around them, the reciprocation, hopefully, will be for that person to pass the same on to the next party, and as things begin to change for the better.

* * *

Cialdini points out "The Hare Krishna Society is an Eastern religious sect with century-old roots traceable to the Indian city of Calcutta. But its spectacular modern-day story occurred in the late 1970s when it experienced a remarkable growth not only in followers but also in wealth and prosperity. The economic growth was funded through a variety of activities, the principal and most visible of which is the request for donations by Society members from passersby in public places. Although most people are threatened by the way the Krishna dress or differences in religion or not having insight into the Krishna, the Krishna found a way to break through the barrier. They offer you a gift. Whether it be a rose or a card, they found that the art of giving is usually followed by a sort of reciprocation."

* * *

If you reach out to others in your actions, perhaps they might reciprocate and become more aware of their own actions and teach others to do the same. Spread the word of integrity.

In this life, we have to make many choices. Some are very important choices. Some are not. Many of our choices are between good and evil. The choices we make, however, determine to a large extent our happiness or our unhappiness, because we have to live with the consequences of our choices.
James E. Faust

* * *

A man does what he must— in spite of personal consequences, in spite of obstacles and dangers and pressures— and that is the basis of all human morality.
Winston Churchill

* * *

We have an innate desire to endlessly learn, grow, and develop. We want to become more than what we already are. Once we yelled to the inclination for a continuous and never-ending improvement, we lead a life of endless accomplishments and satisfaction.
Chuck Gallozzi, The 3 Thieves and 4 Pillars of Happiness

* * *

The consequences of deceit are usually greater than the ones of truth.
Dr. Henry Cloud

Consequences

Do you believe that it should be your responsibility to bring it to the attention of someone when they don't tell the truth and got caught in a lie? If a person is true to themselves, shouldn't they feel some sense of wrongdoing? Perhaps they are trapped in the habit of believing their own deceptions and are not aware of the consequences and obvious reasons for truthfulness?

When we find others being deceitful and allow them to continue lying while in our company, it affects our personal integrity. The people we keep in our circles should always be a reflection of who we are. Therefore, by not confronting someone who you know is being untruthful and by allowing them to be in your company, you are degrading your own values. Perhaps you are not directly affected by their deceptions and choose to remain within their circle. It is a choice that you have to make.

Stephen Carter, law professor and attorney in his book, Integrity states,

"In order to build any entity so that it will survive eternity, you must build a strong foundation. We cannot create change overnight, but we can make an impact on this world if we do it little by little. If each one of us strives to be a better person, each person we touch might strive to do the same."

By increasing an awareness of what is destroying our world and reintroducing the good old values, perhaps we can bring back the good old days where there was a sense of respect in our homes for our parents and family members, respect for our teachers, respect for our coworkers and our employers and the companies that we represent. Do you remember when older brothers stuck up for their younger siblings?

When we regognize someone is not being truthful and showing a lack of integrity, signals coming from two places within us: our stomachs and our heart of hearts. You feel signs from your body which dictate to you what is right and what is not right.

To paraphrase my acquaintance, Felice Cantatore, author of *The Rocky Spirit*, "I always want them to see that when you ever get knocked down, you must get up and fight. Life is about new opportunities. If something doesn't happen the way you wanted it to occur, there is always the next round."

In Felice's book, Rocky Balboa had to overcome his inner demons of self- doubt. As I reflect, that is exactly what Pete Cracovaner, my coach and I worked on, overcoming my inner demons in order to achieve success. We read and discussed the *Knight in Rusty* Armor by Robert Fisher, a great short book about the tales of a knight of yore, who needed to get back in touch with reality. This brave knight was always on a quest to help a damsel in distress or to save a kingdom somewhere. He headed out on crusades to conquer new territories while he left his wife and son home. Eventually, he meets up with Merlin, who teaches him a lesson as he sheds his rusty armor. His armor was the front that he put on so he could run away and not have to face staying home with his wife and son. It's a great short story of humility and honor. The knight through this quest finds the key to what matters most.

As Felice tells it, "Rocky became inspired to reclaim his championship desire and spirit." That is something that we all need to do in order to regain strength in what we feel is right or to strive toward that we want. "It seems like when things don't go your way, it's because something better is waiting for you down the road—as long as you keep positive thoughts. Maintain a "go for it!" attitude.

Components of Integrity: Do You Keep Your Promises?

The man who promises everything is sure to fulfill nothing, and everyone who promises too much is in danger of using evil means in order to carry out his promises and is already on the road to perdition.
Carl Jung

* * *

Lewis Smedes, an ordained minister who teaches at Fuller theological seminary, sees promise as a special form of human endeavor. In a beautiful sermon entitled The Power of Promises, he explains, "When a person makes a promise, he stretches himself out into circumstances that no one can control and controls at least one thing: he will be there no matter what the circumstances turn out to be." A promise, in other words, isn't an open and unequivocal statement about how one intends to live; if sincerely made, it is also a claim of the importance of particular choice that is promised. The ability to promise and then to keep a promise is an aspect simply of liberty but of humanity. "A free self-knows he becomes a genuine self by making commitments to other people— promises he intends to keep even when keeping them exacts a price."

* * *

In executing the duties of my present important station,
I can promise nothing but purity of intentions, and in
carrying these into effect, fidelity and diligence.
George Washington

Passion

Enthusiasm is one of the most powerful engines of success.
When you do a thing, do it with all your might.
Put your whole soul into it. Stamp it with your own personality.
Be active, be energetic, be enthusiastic and faithful, and
you will accomplish your object. Nothing great was ever
achieved without enthusiasm. Ralph Waldo Emerson

* * *

The dictionary says that passion is "a strong emotion, an ardent love, zeal, eager desire, hope and joy." It has been an observation that in every field of endeavor, the men and women who reach the mountain tops of life have a passion to give their all, to be the best they can be. Passion is positive, controllable, and tremendously energizing. The person with a passion for what he or she does becomes a peak performer.

When you share your passion for improvement and for the things you believe in, such as integrity, other people will develop this passion too. It seems as though passion can be contagious. Perhaps we need to spread more passion.

Discipline

The discipline you learn and character you build from setting and achieving a goal can be more valuable than the achievement of the goal itself.
Bo Bennett, Year to Success

* * *

True discipline isn't on your back, needling you with imperatives. It is at your side, nudging you with incentives. These are better pictures because they are true and because they truly build hope for the future.
Sybil Stanton

* * *

The dictionary defines discipline as "to instruct or educate, to inform the mind, to prepare by instructing in correct principles and habits; to advance and prepare my instruction." Integrity requires discipline. It is not something that occurs some of the time, but through discipline, you can drive it deeper into your life. Through practicing something over and over again, we create habits, and integrity is nothing more than good habits that follow individuals and society as a whole. Discipline can make a difference.

As Stephen L. Carter in his book *Integrity* puts it,

> When children of my generation did wrong, they knew it was wrong. Today's kids do not. But if they do not, it may not be because they lack the capacity to choose between good and evil; it may be because they lack the knowledge of the possibility of choice. For this, one can only fault the societal institutions that should, one hopes, facilitate and improve this discerning faculty.

> We should set an example for our children. We should be the role models for generations to come, for if we do not, we will be overrun by a society of random unruliness.

Consciousness

When you look in the mirror, what do you see?
Do you see the real you or what you have
been conditioned to believe is you?
The two are so, so different.
One is an infinite consciousness capable of
being and creating whatever it chooses,
the other is an illusion imprisoned by its own
perceived and programmed limitations.
David Icke

* * *

Consciousness is the quality or state of awareness, the ability to experience or to feel wakefulness, having a sense of selfhood, and the executive control system of the mind.

Consciousness has to do with the development of social responsibility. It is something which begins in child rearing.

Most decisions that we make are conscious and calculated or premeditated. We have the ability to make choices based on alternatives. Every choice is limited to one or more possibilities as of things, propositions, or courses of action, the selection of which precludes any other possibility unlike any other animal.

Subconscious

Anything that we are aware of at a given moment forms part
of our consciousness, making conscious experience at once
the most familiar and most mysterious aspect of our lives.
Max Velmans and Susan Schneider
The Blackwell Companion to Consciousness

Consciousness is based on experiences and the awareness of things that occur, whereas, the subconscious is the totality of mental processes of which the individual is not aware. In Freud's opinion the unconscious mind has a will and purpose of its own that cannot be known to the conscious mind (hence the term "unconscious") and is a repository for socially unacceptable ideas, wishes or desires, traumatic memories, and painful emotions put out of mind by the mechanism of psychological repression.

The subconscious mind stores information that the conscious
mind may not immediately process with full understanding,
but it stores the information for later retrieval when "recalled"
by the conscious mind, or by an astute psychoanalyst who
can draw out information stored in the subconscious,
bringing it to the individual's conscious awareness.
Ezechial Saad

Entitlement

I think that there's something in the American psyche, it's almost this kind of right or privilege, this sense of entitlement, to resolve our conflicts with violence. There's an arrogance to that concept, if you think about it. To actually have to sit down and talk, to listen, to compromise, that's hard work.
Michael Moore

* * *

One of the things that I wonder about often is the difference between the consciousness of ownership and the feeling of entitlement. Entitlement can be the feeling or belief that you deserve to be given something, such as special privileges or, in clinical psychology and psychiatry, an unrealistic, exaggerated, or rigidly held sense of entitlement may be considered a symptom of narcissistic personality disorder, seen in those who "[Freud said] because of early frustrations, they arrogate to themselves the right to demand lifelong reimbursement from fate."

Out of the Fog, an organization that supports families of loved ones who suffer from personality disorders, defines "sense of entitlement" as an unrealistic, unmerited, or inappropriate expectation or favorable living conditions and favorable treatment at the hands of others.

So now that we might have a better understanding of passion, discipline, entitlement, consciousness, and subconscious, these are my thoughts on how one relates to the other. Although when I began this project it was strictly as a monetary ploy for personal gain. I created product to sell. When I began to write about the descriptions of my products, I had an epiphany. The more I wrote, the more I began to read and research the many windows of integrity. It became a mission, as I became compelled to share a message rather than being interested in creating a business for monetary gain. It became a passion of mine to write this book and to begin talking to groups of people. Through me, I am hoping that we can generate a new culture or revive the lack of care, which has developed over this generation and generations to come. If there is a consciousness in our actions and we discipline ourselves properly, our subconscious will take over, and that's when our conscious actions become subconscious actions. A habit develops from within. A total expression of entitlement has arisen in the younger generation. Most of that is learned from their parents or role models and, as I have alluded to previously, has to do with technology and the creation of instant gratification in today's society. Too many people feel that they are entitled to jump a line, throw garbage out their car windows, or park in a fire zone or handicapped parking spot because they are in a hurry.

It pisses me off when people ignore the simple things like throwing paper towels in the garbage pail and not next to it or picking them up and putting them in the pail if they miss, not cleaning the snow off your windows and roof before driving their car, or motoring their way through stop signs without even slowing down or something senseless like throwing garbage out of a car window.

* * *

The longer I live, the more I realize the impact of attitude
on life. Attitude, to me, is more important than facts.
It is more important than the past, than education,
than money, than circumstances, than failures, than
successes, then with other people say or do. It is more
important than appearance, gifted ability, or skill. It
will make or break a company, a church, a home.

Attitude Makes the Difference

The remarkable thing is we have a choice everyday regarding the attitude we will embrace from that day. We cannot change our past, we cannot change the fact that people will act in a certain way. We cannot change the inevitable. The only thing that we can do is play on the one string that we have, and this string is attitude. I am convinced in life is ten percent what happens to me and ninety percent how I react to it. And so it is with you.
We Are in Charge of Our Attitudes by Charles Swindoll

* * *

In the same way, we need to adjust our attitudes to realize that our actions and the actions we portray to others is an entrée to what life is all about, not just a single action, but a total attitude.

Are we too busy?

No time to distinguish right from wrong?

It is not always easy doing the right thing from the heart, but when you are moved to do it, do it no matter what others may think.

In this day of instant gratification and busy schedules, the American society (in particular) has become too busy and no longer pays attention to what might matter most, and that is the difference between right and wrong. Most other cultures have much stricter rules that must be followed or the punishment is far greater than the reward. We bring up our children with the words "no" or "you can't do that!" We try to give them proper guidance so that they can survive in our society.

We've all read Dr. Spock, Ann Douglas, William, Martha, Robert and James Sears, Denise Fields, Jenn Berman, Hal Runkel and Harvey Karp, and many of the thousands of books on child-rearing and child psychology. We experiment on the different styles of training in order to make our children healthier both physically and mentally. As I have seen some parents reprimanding or scolding their children in public places, I wonder if they have ever stopped and thought about the repercussions of their own actions and the messages they are sending their children. Sometimes, I wonder if they realize that children usually copycat what their parents do.

When we talk of bullying, could it stem from stimuli or reactions that children obtain from mocking their parents? After all, your parent is always right!

Family—Raising Children

As Doctor Spock puts it, **"Raising children is more and more puzzling for many parents because we've lost a lot of our old-fashioned convictions about what kind of morals, ambitions, and character we want them to have."**

* * *

We are uncertain and worried about what kind of world awaits our children when they become adults. The pace of social change is almost overwhelming. We can barely keep up with the latest dangers and opportunities for our children's well-being: drugs, violence, the information superhighway, the list seems endless.

Doctor Spock says, "In an uncertain world with more uncertainty to come, we will do well to ask ourselves just what our goals are in raising our children. Is doing well in school our most important objective for them? Is the ability to sustain intimate human relationships more important? Do we want them to be individualistic with a competitive edge so they can succeed in a dog-eat-dog society? Or do we want them to learn to cooperate and sometimes to renounce their own desires for the good of others? If the ultimate goal of raising children is the fashioning of a fully formed adult, then just what kind of person do we want that adult to be in order to be a happy and productive member of society?"

These questions cut to the heart of much of raising children. Parenting is about choices. In order to decide what's best for your child, you will always be well served to step back and think about these tough questions before making a decision. So many parents get totally caught up in the difficult day-to-day issues of how they are parenting that they lose perspective about why they are parenting in the first place. I hope that raising your children will help you to understand your own ideas about what's really important to you in life and that this insight will guide the choices you make about raising your child.

When it comes to teaching your children how to possess integrity, you can only sow the seeds to give them the opportunity to form this characteristic. They grow to be individuals; they grow to have their own wants and desires. You can only hope you've instilled enough knowledge and self-belief that they use these tools to show integrity.

Alan Goodwin, in an article titled "Infecting Your Kids with Integrity", published on Aug 20, 2007, writes, "It's not who you are in life that matters," a famous American father told his later-to-be-famous sons. "It's who people think you are." When a person adopts this way of thinking, a split develops between the public and private, with more emphasis being placed on image management than character development. A person of integrity, on the other hand, values consistency. That is, he strives to be the same in private as he is in public. He is who he appears to be. His private behavior matches the public perception. He's the real deal.

* * *

How do we raise kids who possess integrity in a culture that seems to value image more than character? Like many things, integrity is more often caught than taught. There are at least three ways to infect our kids with integrity.

Dr. Henry Cloud puts it: If we work too hard to instill a sense of unwavering right and wrong in our children: in effect they might grow into adults who will have difficulty reaching any moral conclusions other than the ones into which they have been trained.

We get so caught up in our own world that we forget what is most important, our families. Are we out playing golf on the weekends instead of taking our kids on a family outing? Do we attend business functions and miss family dinners? Are we avoiding our families because of distractions that we allow to take us over? Do we stop and think about what's right and wrong? Did we stop being good role models for our children? What kind of role models did we become?

Professor and author Howard Hendricks said, "You cannot impart what you do not possess." If we don't demonstrate personal integrity, our kids will never catch the infection.

What about those times when we blow it? When our inconsistencies display themselves? The discomfort of that inclines us to engage in cover-ups, to pretend, or to act as though the blooper never happened.

In the wake of a mistake, we have the opportunity to teach our kids something else very important about integrity. That is, when we blow it (which we will), we need to acknowledge it, take responsibility for it, and correct it. This keeps us off the slippery slope populated by integrity-deficient people, where mistake-free portrayals are commonplace. Personal integrity is hurt not by errors but by refusing to acknowledge them. Politicians are sometimes told, "The public tolerates confession better than deception."

When we confide in our children, it is important to have them understand what is appropriate to discuss in public (with friends or family outside the inner circle). They need to understand what can and what cannot be said in the company of strangers so that outside or public opinion does not affect the inner workings of the private rule. "The person you are in private should match the person you are in public." That's integrity.

If we, as parents, demonstrate consistency, acknowledging personal flaws and encouraging openness, the integrity we seek to instill is attainable in a culture hungry for authentic, real-deal people.

* * *

Tony Chen wrote in "Raising Kids of Strong Character: Integrity": As a parent, teaching your child how to act with integrity is vital for their development. You don't want your child to become a person who breaks promises, lies, and has no concern for others. After all, you're raising a child, not a politician... It's up to you to teach your kids about integrity. If you don't, the media and their friends will teach them completely opposite values. Think of it as a non-violent fight between you and "them" for your child's character, values, and traits. By being an example and using the mentioned suggestions, you're much more likely to win the fight. The important thing is that you give it your best shot and hope for the best. Even our best efforts can fail, but no effort at all is certain to fail indeed.

* * *

Abraham Lincoln on Child-Rearing from "Abraham Lincoln Speaks: 'The Fate of Humanity Is in the Hands of the Child" by Taiwo Akinlami, February 2, 2013

A child is a person who is going to carry on what you have started. He is going to sit where you're sitting and when you're gone, attend to those things, which are important. You may adopt all the policies you please, but how they are carried out depends on him. He will assume control of your cities, states, and nation. He is going to move in and take over your churches, schools, universities and corporations. The fate of humanity is in his hands.

A Letter from Abraham Lincoln to His Son's Teacher:

My son starts school today. It is all going to be strange and new to him for a while and I wish you would treat him gently. It is an adventure that might take him across continents. All adventures that probably include wars, tragedy, and sorrow. To live this life will require faith, love and courage.

So dear Teacher, will you please take him by his hand and teach him things he will have to know, teaching him—but gently, if you can. Teach him that for every enemy, there is a friend. He will have to know that all men are not just, that all men are not true. But teach him also that for every scoundrel there is a hero, that for every crooked politician, there is a dedicated leader.

Teach him if you can that 10 cents earned is of far more value than a dollar found. In school, teacher, it is far more honorable to fail than to cheat. Teach him to learn how to gracefully lose, and enjoy winning when he does win. Teach him to be gentle with people, tough with tough people. Steer him away from envy if you can and teach

49

him the secret of quiet laughter. Teach him if you can—how to laugh when he is sad, teach him there is no shame in tears. Teach him there can be glory in failure and despair in success. Teach him to scoff at cynics. Teach him if you can the wonders of books, but also give time to ponder the extreme mystery of birds in the sky, bees in the sun and flowers on a green hill. Teach him to have faith in his own ideas, even if everyone tells him they are wrong.

Try to give my son the strength not to follow the crowd when everyone else is doing it. Teach him to listen to everyone, but teach him also to filters all that he hears on a screen of truth and take only the good that comes through. Teach him to sell his talents and brains to the highest bidder but never to put a price tag on his heart and soul. Let him have the courage to be impatient, let him have the patient to be brave. Teach him to have sublime faith in himself, because then he will always have sublime faith in mankind, in God.

This is the order, teacher, but see what best you can do. He is such a nice little boy and he is my son.

So much is written about how the lack of integrity is hurting our children and our families, but it hurts our own morality just as much. "If we decide that we do not have the time to stop and think about right and wrong, then we do not have the time to figure out right and wrong, which means we do not have the time to live according to our model of right and wrong, which means that we do not have time for a life of integrity."

I keep repeating throughout this book that we are the role models that our children mock. We want them to grow up to be people of good morals and react in a manner that we trained them.

Marriage

Husbands, love your wives well. You are teaching your sons how they should treat a woman and you are teaching your daughters what they should expect of a man.
Author Unknown

Stephen Carter, Law Professor and attorney, in his book Integrity, speaks about the wedding vow. He says, "according to a tradition, is a promise under God and is made in the name of God. When kept, a marriage is a beautiful institution that our children also learn from. Marriage is a civilizing institution, a means of curbing desires or inclinations that might have otherwise made social stability impossible. Lately, though, the institution of marriage is entered into with such lack of integrity, whereas, one takes a vow for life and forsakes a moral commitment that one has made for all eternity."

In America, the average marriage lasts for only a part of one's life. The divorce rate is around 50 percent, and 50 percent of the marriages that fail, resulting in 50 percent more remarriages that once again fail.

When people take an oath to be married "in the eyes of God", they pledged to love, honor, and cherish one another in sickness and in health till death do they part.

Carter proposes: What happens in the case where one of the spouses stops loving and cherishing, and as a result, the other spouse becomes unfaithful and goes outside of the marriage to do an adulterous activity? Who is the dis-integritous party? Is it the spouse who went outside of the marriage or is it the spouse that stopped loving and cherishing, which was the cause for the other spouse to go outside of the marriage to fulfill a need that had been revoked by the other partner?

When marriage becomes only a contract and loses its value as an institution, I believe, due to the lack of communication, a couple of things should occur.

The first is that they need to start communicating and find out what went wrong and/or to seek assistance by going to a marriage counselor or similar entity before things get too far out of hand. It's true that nobody is totally sure of what it means to be married until you have been there for a while.

People change, circumstances change. It has become too easy to get a divorce today, and too easy for people to lose the idea of commitment.

What is your level of integrity when it comes to your marriage?

Teaching with Integrity

These are challenging times for education. The public holds schools and teachers more accountable for student learning as demonstrated by everyone's expectations for stronger student's performances on standardized tests and higher graduation rates. Unfortunately, the increased emphasis on reading, mathematics and science, to prepare students for a global, technological, and information-based marketplace, seems to relegate the general wellbeing have students to a low educational priority.

Teachers can and should serve as role models who teach character and moral values. Teachers who demonstrate integrity are accountable for providing academic programs of quality and positive educational experiences.

A teacher's integrity, or lack thereof, is observed by students. Students' evaluation of the character of the teacher is based on how they are treated and taught. Students know when the teachers are committed to their psychomotor, cognitive, and affective learning, and they can tell when that teachers genuinely cares about them and are trustworthy, honest, and respectful, how teachers can serve as role models by teaching character and the moral virtues of honesty, trust, fairness, respect, and responsibility.

Teachers should emphasize the importance of exercising self-control and restraint when challenged and should respond appropriately so students act fairly and justly, and therefore, they would not bully others if bullying occurs. Students must be instructed on fairness, respect, and responsibility, so they will know how to behave more appropriately toward others.

Lessons learned inside the classroom and through teacher-student interactions outside of the classroom should be based on the virtues of integrity, honesty, trust, fairness, respect, and responsibility. These should characterize teachers and their relationships with students. Teachers with character deal honestly with students in a trustworthy manner and nurture mutual trust and respect.

Teachers with character teach their students that individuals make moral and principal decisions through the moral-reasoning process. They can help their students know what their values are, believe in these values as an integral part of who they are, and live their life in alignment with these values. Teachers can play an essential role in helping students learn and apply a moral-reasoning process.

I am so proud that my son Michael has made such marvelous strides in making an impact on the world of education. His values are in alignment with the true value of education. I asked him if he would like to write a piece for my book and here is his response, "In this time when teachers are constantly being asked to do things that violate our commitment to our students (i.e., forcing kindergarteners and preschoolers to take standardized tests instead of learning by playing, telling kids they can't flush the toilet during testing time, etc.), it's tough to maintain one's integrity, be true to one's own beliefs, and still be a 'good employee.'"

* * *

Article: Named one of the top 50 educators in the world, the curriculum coach at WSES:

Michael Soskil was in line to win the Global Teacher Prize. Sponsored by the Varkey Foundation, the Global Teacher Prize is a $1 million award that has been called the Nobel Prize for teachers. If given the chance, Soskil said students can change the world. Last year, WSES fourth grade students worked with students in India, to stop child labor practices in Asia and Africa. Through such projects, Soskil said the students see what can be done because they were part of the operation and the story isn't simply coming from something a teacher is saying. Soskil spent the first year of his career teaching in Arizona, later moving back to teach at his alma mater. Now, 17 years later he has received a list of recognitions that include the Presidential Award for Excellence in Teaching last year and most recently, in November Soskil was named the Microsoft Innovative Educator Expert. After receiving each award, Soskil has said he doesn't do his job for the recognition. He did say, however, being named in the top 50 is exciting because it recognizes the innovation that is occurring at WSES. The Global Teacher Prize is different than Soskil's previous awards, he said, because this award is about promoting the profession of teaching globally, exposing students to world issues and showing them what is possible in the world. Unlike past awards, where he was nominated, Soskil applied for the Global Teacher Prize because of suggestions from some of his associates. Proud of all that is happening at WSES, Soskil said that the reason he applied was that he saw it as an opportunity to "share what we're doing on a global stage." The application was submitted in October and he learned of his placement in December. Soskil must wait until February to see if he is named to the top-10 list, which he admits is making him anxious. If named to the top 10, Soskil will travel to Dubai where the winner will be announced at the Global Education and Skills Forum in March. (Unfortunately did not move further) Competing against educators from 127 countries, Soskil said he is honored because he sees himself as the messenger that shares the experiences that occur at WSES. The teachers he works with are special, he said, because of their commitment to providing innovative education. He feels this is unique, he said. He explained that the WSES teachers aren't satisfied with doing what has been done before and as a result, they look for "new ways to make education special for kids and to bring exceptional experiences." (Katie Collins, News Eagle, January 2, 2015)

Michael was nominated again for the Global Teacher Prize in 2016. He placed in the top 10 and for many reasons that would have been politically incorrect, he did not place First.

Students deserve teachers who offer a genuine piece of themselves and are more interested in conveying real knowledge than just filling a career. The performance of teachers directly affects, molds, and structures the life of children or students. I praise all of those teachers who really care about the impact they make.

Excellence and Ethics: Academic Integrity, A Critical Challenge for Schools

One of the tools with which to combat the Ego is to open ourselves up to being humiliated. In this way, the ego takes a hike and the Light of our soul which is usually covered up by our ego gets to shine. Welcome humiliation! It helps you to see the Light inside of who you really are. Moments of embarrassment are just moments of accelerated change.
Yahuda Berg

A high school student on a cheating scandal: "This world has become very competitive, and cheaters sometimes win. I study so hard, and it's a real slap in the face when I see kids cheating and scoring higher grades than me on a test and getting away with it."

* * *

Academic Integrity: A Critical Challenge for Schools by David Wangaard and Jason Stephens

Our schools are facing a crisis of academic integrity. In our recent three-year study of academic motivation and integrity, we surveyed over 3,600 students from six economically and ethnically diverse high schools in the northeastern United States. Ninety-five percent of these students reported engaging in at least one form of academic cheating during the past academic year. More troubling still, 57% of these students also agreed or strongly agreed with the statement, "It is morally wrong to cheat." While academic dishonesty may not be the gravest moral problem facing our youth, it is certainly the most ubiquitous. Practiced habitually, cheating becomes, for moral character, a kind of "death by a thousand tiny cuts." In our study, 44% of students reported seeing test cheating weekly; 82% reported seeing homework cheating weekly. But only 12% of students reported seeing others being caught cheating in any given week. The failure of schools to enforce their academic integrity standards may be one reason why only 11% of students in our study expressed support for their schools' academic integrity policies.

* * *

It was in 2011 when high school students in Great Neck, New York, a relatively high-income community where children have been extended liberties and opportunities way beyond those that the average child could possibly expect in a lifetime. These kids travel and go on lavish vacations, they drive fancy cars, attend sporting events and concerts in front-row seats. They have been given a free reign to go first class in every aspect of their lives. They have opportunities that most working people cannot afford.

I guess I am just exemplifying this group because they got caught cheating on the SATs, not to say students from every other area, as well as adults alike, don't cheat on exams that are used for employment testing, placement, advancement, or job security. However, these were students come from wealthy, successful families. This is not to say that they don't have other pressures to succeed or be confronted with the disappointment and disgrace that they cause their families if they don't succeed. What values have these wealthy, successful people given to their children? Is it that you need to cheat to win?

Another issue here is in regard to entitlement. Do these students feel entitled to cheat because of their parent's financial status? Have they been born into a culture that has given them the right to cheat?

Role Models

*It's amazing what happens when you recognize your good
qualities, accept responsibility for your future, and take
positive action to make that future even brighter."*
Zig Zigler

* * *

One of the greatest impacts on my life come from the principles I
attained from reading Zig Zigler

Zig Ziglar died in November 2012 at the age of eighty-six. A World
War II veteran, he became the top sales person in several organizations
before striking out on his own as a motivational speaker and trainer.
With a Southern charm and lessons grounded in Christianity, Ziglar
wrote over two dozen books and amassed a following of millions who
were encouraged by his lessons for success.

Banned for Life

In an interview of actor Ted Danson with Cal Fussman on September
10, 2010, Ted Danson said, "Integrity is what you feel and know on
the inside matches what you say and do on the outside. Courage is

something I don't know how much I have. You can't plan for it. You either do the right thing or you don't when the moment comes. If you've got integrity, it will smack you when you fuck it up. If you don't have integrity, you'll go on for a very long time beating the crap out of people, robbing, stealing, and there's nothing inside you that tells what you're doing is wrong. Life won't even bother to slap you."

Although there are people like Zig Zigler, who make a positive impression for the betterment of all, there are also those who, to our surprise, deceive and can make a very negative impact as well.

Take a look at the current role models in sports alone. In "The Greatest Deception in World Sports," Lance Armstrong, seven-time Tour de France winner, finally admitted to the world that he was taking enhancement drugs. Here's someone that we, along with our children and the rest of the world, took in as a hero and role model. A man fighting cancer who became a "winner." Does that send a message to our kids that enhancement drugs (or any drugs) make you a winner? Is this an acceptable thing?

How many people did he let down? What are the repercussions for the competitors that might have finished first? The anti-hero changed many lives. He has let down his fans, he has lost all of his recognition, and his reputation is tarnished forever. His integrity is banished. When given the opportunity to come clean six months before, he could have. He would not have faced as much disgrace then as he will now. The question he faces, which came out in an interview with Oprah Winfrey, is did his doping cause his cancer? As it is, Lance Armstrong now faces millions of dollars in lawsuits from the federal government. He deceived people by replacing his slogan of Live Long, Live Strong to Live Strong, Lie Long. What is going to be his ride to redemption now?

Mark Spitz, an Olympic swimmer, and gold medal winner admitted he took performance drugs to Michael Phelps, all-time gold medal swimming champion, who had a photo appear showing him smoking marijuana through a bong.

Alex Rodriquez, the Yankee hero, after testifying several times, was suspended for a year for lying about his using steroids. Is he the "great" role model we want our children to believe in?

Ray Rice, a football player for the Baltimore Ravens, punches his fiancé in an elevator and gets caught on camera. The NFL suspends him for games. Sponsors pull their advertising.

Adrian Peterson, running back and star of the Minnesota Vikings, was sighted swishing his young child with a branch and subsequently breaking his son's skin to teach his son a lesson. He was also caught in pictures. It was his first assault, battery, or domestic violence offense and faced a six-game suspension and loss of pay for the balance of the season. Advertisers pulled out from local and national advertising campaigns to keep from getting negative identification of their products from the public. At least we can see that major advertisers are recognizing that the public opinion counts and the integrity of their products and corporate brands need to be protected.

What about Charlie Sheen, from his first appearance in Ferris Bueller's Day Off and later becoming a huge star in Two and a Half Men until his meltdown following his rehabilitation for drug and alcohol abuse and marital problems stemming from abuse and allegations of domestic violence, was a household star. His outlandish statements during television interviews and outrageous videos that he posted on YouTube, as well as his cursing out of former employers, publicly cost him his role in Two and a Half Men.

What Is an Integrity Commitment?

Olympic athletes pay the price. I learned that the only way you're going to get anywhere in life is to work hard at it. Whether you are a musician, writer, an athlete, or a businessman, there is no getting around it. If you do, you'll win; if you don't, you won't.
Bruce Jenner, Olympic gold medalist in the decathlon

Athletes Whose Commitment Means More

Taking on the role of a professional athlete has its perks and it has its pitfalls. When you take on a role as a professional, you have a full understanding that you are playing to win and aggressively play your best just as your opponents, other professionals, whose intent is to play hard and win. Yes, you experience injuries along the way, but whose responsibility is it when you accept the role? After all: A golfer could get hit by a stray ball.

Sandy Kofax, Hall of Famer LA Dodger's star pitcher, refused to pitch in the World Series, on Yom Kippur, the holiest day of the Jewish New Year. By not taking the mound for the Dodgers against the Twins on October 6, 1965, on the Day of Atonement, the holiest day on the Jewish calendar, he became a cultural touchstone. Koufax, who wasn't particularly observant, had no clue that his decision would carry so much weight then or now. "I believe he was thinking, 'I'm going to pitch the next day. What's the big deal? Yom Kippur is a day of sacrifice....And here's Koufax, who's doing this reflexively, not out of his own great belief, but really more in deference to others. So it was a much greater sacrifice on his part. For a more religious man, it might have been a no-brainer. For Koufax, it was the right thing to do." And in doing the right thing, Koufax inspired a generation of Jewish players that came after him.

After training to be the greatest runner of his time, in the movie Chariots of Fire, Little, a Jewish Englishman, refused to run in the Olympics on a Saturday because it is his Sabbath, and out of respect to his religious beliefs, if he ran, he would have been sacrificing his religious integrity.

* * *

Not as well-known as many others, Eric Liddell, a great missionary and Olympic champion and an incredible athlete, so strongly held on to what he believed to be right. He said, "When I run, I feel God's pleasure."

One of the reasons why Eric Liddell is an extraordinary hero is because he refused to run on a Sunday. When he heard that the first Olympic 100-meter race was to be held on that day, he boldly said, "I'm not running." He believed that that day was special, and he never had run on a Sunday before. So instead of being on the track that Sunday with all of the other racers, Eric was at church. His country called him a traitor, and it seemed like the world had turned its back on him, but Eric onto his beliefs even to the point that the Prince of Wales begged him to change his mind! Eric's resolution not to run was so strong that he turned down the prince's pleadings, as well as that of his own country.

He too was a hero because he was not afraid to stand up for what he believed was right. Eric also showed perseverance in always trying to do his best till the very end. I think that these are some of the characteristics that make a person a true hero.

On the year 2014, a New York Yankee legend retired. He is Derek Jeter, the Man of the Year. In an article in Celebrity Fitness, Derek Jeter talks about his evolution as a leader, how he's fueled by doubters, and why integrity is so damn important.

The lack of pretension is disarming. Derek Jeter, 1996 Rookie of the Year, the eleven-time All-Star, the five-time World Champion, and the guy joined the 3000-hit club early in the 2011 season, just before he hit thirty-seven years old is considered one of the greatest Yankees, and is a first-ballot Hall of Fame to be sure. He says, "It's all about patience, control of the situation, and control of yourself." At every level, it seemed like the game was faster. The bigger the situation, the more the game speeds up. That's all mental. It messes people up. You think, "I've got to do this, I've got to do that, when in reality, all you have to do is the same thing you've always been doing. Slow it down. Realize you've been in this situation before. You've been successful in this situation before. Be calm. The more you can do that, the more pressure you take off yourself, and the easier it is to perform.

That's part of what made Derek Jeter officially inspiring although the inspiration depends on the context. There is no denying that the guy played hard, led the team, showed class, and never used his mouth as a firearm. Reputations like this do not happen by accident. "Obviously, you're known for what you do," says Jeter. "But you still want to be known as a good person. You're a person a lot longer before and after you're a professional athlete. People always say to me, 'Your image is this, your image is that.' Your image isn't your character. Character is what you are as a person. That's what I worried about."

* * *

New York Mets: Why David Is the "Wright" Choice for Captain by Jason Lempter*, March 21, 2013

What makes a good captain? Well, a captain is one who can lead by example. He (or she) knows the right ways to go, the right things to do. A captain doesn't buckle under pressure; more, a captain thrives under pressure.

Wright provides his interpretation of the role he has inherited: "I think that the responsibilities are kind of the same as what I've always tried to do," he added. "I'm not a real 'rah rah,' yell and scream kind of guy...I think it's more lead by example. I'm going to take the responsibility seriously and with a great deal of pride." Wright meets the qualifications of being a captain and was recently dubbed "Captain America" by his teammates on Team USA during a recent installment of the World Baseball Classic, where Wright led all participants with 10 RBI.

First of all, he has the notable stats and achievements that warrant such an honor. Over his eleven Major League seasons (all with the Mets), Wright owns a .298 batting average, more than 200 home runs and over 170 stolen bases. He's a seven-time All-Star and has two Gold Gloves for his stellar play at third base.

Wright owns top honors in Mets' franchise history in a number of offensive categories, including runs scored, hits, total bases, most extra-base hits, doubles and RBI and most walks and runs close second to Darryl Strawberry's 252 HR's.

Additionally, Wright has been, and will continue to be around for a while. Just about ever since Wright arrived in Flushing, he had "leader" written all over him. In 2008, then-manager Jerry Manuel called on Wright to take leadership of the team after Carlos Delgado had gone down with an injury. Wright didn't take long to answer the call. Wright was humble enough to publicly play down the assignment, as he didn't wish to upset any of the veterans on the club. But Wright was a born leader in the Mets clubhouse.

What makes David Wright "Captain"? It is the integrity he has for the fans, his reputation for living the truth and having good character. *Lempter is a columnist who features athletes who refuse to play out of religious convictions.

Integrity in Our Personal Lives— What Controls Your Life?

Real integrity is doing the right thing, knowing that nobody's going to know whether you did it or not.
Oprah Winfrey

* * *

I try to demonstrate integrity in every part of my daily life from the time I get up in the morning till the time I fall asleep at night. It is about a commitment toward doing each and everything you do in the best manner you possibly can. It's thinking about whether or not you could be doing things better. Simple things like considering the way you brush your teeth, the way you kiss your spouse in the morning, how you treat others on a line at Dunkin' Donuts, holding the door for a stranger, working out at the gym, and cleaning the machines after you use them. I think about the way I make my bed by tucking in every corner, whether I close a draw all the way. I guess you might be getting the message; however, I attach passion to integrity because, if you are considerate about the smaller things in life, you will become more aware of how to deal with the bigger things. They all make a difference.

Although nobody comes into our bedroom other than my wife and me, and it wouldn't make any difference to anyone other than my wife and me, our bed is made every morning(even when she's away on a business trip). If the corners were not tucked, no one would ever notice; however, my mother taught me that the way you begin your day is to make your bed first thing in the morning, and the rest of your day will follow and be more organized.

Is it you and your inner self or is it others and outside influences that drive you to make the decisions that you make?

What are the little things that drive you?

These are some of the things I have noticed lacking in our current society that need to be addressed, and I guess that's why I began writing in the first place.

I learned it's the little things in life that can lead to the bigger things in life as I bring more and more things into my inner consciousness. I continue to be more aware of the impact each decision I make on my family, my neighbors, my associates, and the world. If everyone increased their overall consciousness about the way we live, even if it's the slightest bit, there would be a huge impact on ourselves and future generations.

So what pisses me off?

It's the little things that become blatant things later on. We all know that the world is constantly changing and it's becoming more and more frightful when you reflect on everything that's going on in this world.

I work in a very nice office building. In the suites that I share with other people, there is a cafeteria, common kitchen, bathroom, and conference area. I feel that the appearance of my surroundings is a reflection on who I am or who my clients perceive me to be. There are little things, such as intentionally being shortchanged, paper towels thrown on the floor in a public bathroom, or dirty dishes left in the sink. Do these things matter? Why is it that I feel the urge to pick up after someone else's mess?

If we ignore all the little things, if we're okay telling the little white lies, where does this end? And what kind of resolve can we expect unless we correct them?

Should you lie to avoid hurting your parents' feelings, protect your kids from a frightening truth, or keep a dying man from knowing his fate?

How about speaking a white lie to keep a surprise party secret or exaggerating in an interview to get a job?

Where do you draw the line?

White Lies

Walking Your Talk: The Path of Personal Integrity
CAT THOMPSON · MARCH 2004

To find the roots of our dishonesty within ourselves, we need only look as far as our cultural patterns on language and lies. Most of us consider ourselves good people. We recycle our cardboard, give to charity, and generally try to do the right thing when we have the opportunity. Yet most nice people also lie quite frequently. Why is that? And how has that become acceptable behavior?

The dictionary describes the word "lie" in the following way:

"verb

1. to say something that is not true in a conscious effort to deceive somebody,
2. to give a false impression;

noun

1. a false statement made deliberately,
2. a false impression created deliberately."

In all four of these descriptions, one thing stands out clearly—that lying is something we do deliberately, that our purpose for lying is to intentionally deceive. Obviously, this type of activity seems at odds with being nice. How is it that we can consider ourselves good people and include lying?

We may think our lying is for a good reason: to keep from hurting someone's feelings, to smooth over conflict, or to make someone happy. After all, what does it hurt to tell a little white lie every once in a while? What lying does, as a rule, is to create multiple realities. When you lie, reality splits; it disintegrates. You now have one reality that you know and live in, knowing the truth about a particular issue as well as the reality that the people—to whom you've lied to—live in, which is designed around somewhat, or totally, different information.

The people to whom you have lied to make decisions and choices based on the reality they inhabit, but it's a different reality than the one you inhabit so that split will now influence your relationship and your common future.

Presumably, you told the white lie to make these other people's reality nicer, but you probably also told it to make your reality more comfortable (i.e., by lying, you avoided feeling bad, disappointing them, or being the bearer of bad news). The problem is you are creating this potentially huge disintegration without having any real way of knowing what the repercussions of that reality-split will be down the road. You can't know how this separate reality might circle back in the future, and you can't really know whether the net outcome for this other person will be better or worse than the course of the reality that might have resulted if you had told the truth. All you can know for sure is that you've now created a rift in a continuum of both your own and these other people's lives, and you've taken charge, if even in a small way, of designing someone else's reality.

The more lies you tell, of course, the more multiple realities you create and must live with. That's an enormous responsibility, and it can also be energy draining because it literally costs you integrity—the state of being connected, sound, consistent and undivided.

When enough white lies are floating in your midst, your integrity becomes fractured. You may feel pulled in a thousand directions and unable to make decisions without the fear that all these custom-made realities could come crashing down around you. You may also not feel like you fully know or trust yourself at times.

I grew up in a family with parents who thought it was acceptable to tell little white lies. They created the misnomer of "It's okay."

Well, my parents did, so why couldn't we?

First, it started off because you were protecting someone from knowing the truth because they might get hurt from the outcome, that is, for example, Grandma has a bad heart, so she doesn't need to know about so and so; or If I told my mom, she's going to get angry with me; I can't tell my dad because he told me not to do that; and the like.

One time, when I was about eight or nine years old, I got caught stealing exploding caps (about 25 cents at that time) from the neighborhood luncheonette. (We used to take a rock and smash the caps to make them pop and explode or put them under a powerful magnifying glass in the sunlight) It was very embarrassing because my parents owned a store in the same strip shopping center. Harold, the owner of the luncheonette, who I knew well, brought me to my parents store by the collar to tell my parents what I had done. I learned a lesson in humility from that experience. As I grew up, there were times when my parents did little things that made me question the difference between right and wrong. I had mixed messages coming into my control center, my young and susceptible brain; however, I noticed that my conscience was always talking to me and in a flux of confusion. Even today, my father might say, "Don't tell your mom. It will only upset her." I ask, "Why, shouldn't she know?

When Is a Friendship a Real Friendship?

If you go looking for a friend, you're going to find they're scarce.
If you go out to be a friend, you'll find them everywhere.
Zig Zigler

* * *

We have been told that if toward the end of your life you maintain a handful of friends, you are wealthy. People pop in and out of your life for whatever reason. Sometimes you develop great relationships and sometimes they are like fleeting moments, neither here nor there. At times, friendships develop because of the need for companionship, commonalities, loneliness, or greed.

If you're having trouble deciding whether your friend is a true friend, then your relationship must already be rocky. If you want to decide whether your friend is in the friendship for the right reasons, you have to pay attention to what they say, what they do, and how they make you feel.

A true friend should make you feel needed, confident, and better about being alive. If your friend is always putting you down or making you feel worthless and never give you a kind word when you need it, then that friend is not true blue. If you want to know if your friend is a good friend, see if they make comments that encourage you.

You want to be sure you can trust the person you are friends with and that they can keep secrets you choose to share with them, and if not, then friends who do not have honesty or loyalty will become backstabbers or tell secrets to others.

What do you call someone who milks you dry to obtain resources from you and then dumps you like a dead fish? Do you call them a friend?

Sometimes you can recognize this right away. It can take days or weeks, and sometimes it takes years till you find out what someone is really all about.

Have you ever heard the story Pinocchio, a marionette who always uses lies to make others feel sorry for him in order to get personal gain? His fairy godmother appeared and granted him a wish to become a real boy. She makes a deal with him that he must be true and honest. As Pinocchio tells lies, his nose grows which allows everyone around him to detect his lies. Once he realizes he can't live a life of shame and deceit and live his dream, he became honest with himself and others and becomes a real boy. After reading this story, I believe you will understand that in a friendship relationship, honesty is the most important trait one should have. Although many traits such as respectfulness, trustworthiness, and caring are also important to have, one believes that honesty is the number one trait.

To establish a friendship relationship, one should be able to believe in each other. They should be able to trust one another by trusting in their word. Having good intentions speaks about having good character. When someone has good intentions, then someone can be believed in. If we are not honest, people will not believe us anymore, and it will destroy our friendships and our future and no one will believe in what you say anymore.

Circle of Trust:
The Fockers

Who have you chosen to be in your circle of trust, your most trusted circle of trust, your "strategic alliances"?

Jack Byrnes (played by Robert DeNiro), in a confidential meeting bestowing his reluctant blessing on Gregg's engagement to his daughter Pam, says to Gregg Focker (played by Ben Stiller), "With the knowledge, you have been given you are on the inside of the circle of trust. If I can't trust you, once you're out, you're out, and I can't put you back in."

(Draw a circle and put an arrow in the center. That is your circle of trust, then put a dot outside the circle and call it Gregg.)

Every person needs a circle of friends to help in reaching his or her full potential. That's as true for leaders as it is for farmers. If we want to cultivate a life of personal integrity and purpose, we must cultivate relationships that will keep us on track. Every person needs to develop a few close friendships with people who will lovingly hold him or her accountable for keeping life focused and balanced.

You know the old adage, "You can't judge a book by its cover?" The same goes for people.

The people we instantly hit it off with could become our worst enemy while the people we don't always get along with right away are sometimes meant to be our best of friends.

- We may think we know the person in front of us, but we never really know.
- We see the cover, not the soul. Stay open and seek to see the light in everyone.
- Did you ever notice how we make everything all about us?

How many times, when a friend is going through a problem, we immediately go into a story of something similar that happened to us instead of really listening to them and just being a shoulder to lean on? Some of us even busy our minds, trying to find the lesson from their tragedy to help our own lives, so much so that we stop feeling our friend's pain altogether!

We never realize our relationship with the person next to us is at any given moment. We can be sitting next to someone on the bus, and they may be someone we hurt in a past life and owe an apology to, or they can be a messenger sent to change our lives. We can never be sure what the reason is, but we can be sure there is a reason.

Today, be open to everyone you meet. Keep your smile warmed up. And get the word "random" out of your head. As Einstein said, "God doesn't play dice…"

Are you obligated to share sensitive information about your friend with his or her potential employer or spouse? Are you allowed to read information embedded in an electronic file that the sender didn't intend for you to see?

Is it ethical to use a covert nanny cam to protect your children?

How will you decide?

Relationships—Who Wants to Be Single?

My Brother admitted to his wife of 28 years that he had been unfaithful to her. Over a period of 4 years, they lived under the same roof and occasionally they shared dinners and bottles of wine together. They shared romantic interludes (because sex was that good, between them). The concept of being single again was not very appealing, so they continued their charade for years until realization set in. They were not meant to be together for eternity.

Such is the same in an article titled Single Again—Where Did Integrity Go? by Lucy Connor, CNN iReport, CNN.com, June 4, 2014

I have historically been a people pleaser. I am not one to rock the boat, to cause confrontation or partake in verbal volleys. In a phrase, I have a hard time saying no. This particular weakness has been the reason I have not always had the integrity that I now strive for. I have made empty promises to friends, students, my children, and others in my life who asked for things that I wanted to give but was not able to. I was afraid that if I was honest, if I said, "I just cannot do that," I would be rejected. Therefore, I have gone through much of my life with great intentions of doing everything I have promised, but not always following through.

As I have grown older and grown up, I understand more and more what integrity means in relationships. Doing what you say you will do and being who you say you are can be the foundation for all types of relationships. Conversely, making empty claims and promises can kill relationships before they begin.

It seems to me, the online dating phenomenon is bursting with people lacking integrity. Do I think all of these people are bad? Certainly not! Do I think all of these people are good? That is another matter.

Goodness involves character and integrity. When you post photos that you know make you look deceptively awesome or young, when you tell a little white lie about your employment status, when you say you want to be married when you are really looking for a hook-up, you are making the statement that you are not as "good" as you possibly strive to be. Goodness is in how you treat others, lying to them is not a great beginning.

In the old days, a deal was sealed with a good word from a friend and a handshake. People looked each other in the eyes and had "real" friendships. If a friend said he was coming over to eat with you, he came. To do otherwise would show a lack of character, integrity, and trustworthiness. In today's world, people's words are worth as much as the paper they are written on…and since no one writes on paper anymore… I had gone on a couple dates with a guy that appeared to be "promising". He was divorced and his ex-wife had since passed away. He was truly single with little baggage. He loved to travel and was a former teacher. I checked with a mutual friend and she said… be careful, he is a bit of a player. I (knowing everything…) did not heed her words. To me, he was great. For our third or fourth date, we made plans to have dinner at my house. He is retired and I am still working, so in order to cook a decent meal for him, I made it the day before. I whipped up two different vegan dishes that could be easily refrigerated overnight and heated up when I got home from work. I spent a good bit of time and money on this adventure, so imagine my surprise when I got a TEXT and hour before he was to be at my house. He just said he had to cancel. There was no explanation, no follow-up call…nada. About a week later when I still had not been given an apology or explanation, I returned the favor and texted him back saying that apparently he had less character than I had thought and I was no longer interested in seeing him. I am quite sure this was just fine on his part. It was a lesson learned before too much time was spent on this particular relationship. It did tell me once again, to be a little less trusting but also to be a little more trustworthy as I proceed in this process. Getting my head out of the fantasy land of the computer and into real life helps me to be a person with greater character and integrity. If I have to look someone in the eyes, I am more likely to be truthful and honest with him On this strange roller-coaster called Single Again, every day is a new learning experience. I am trying to live, not just pretend to live. I am trying to be a woman of character and expect the men I date to be men of integrity as well. It may just be a pipe dream, but I believe they are still out there…and one is my forever.

Do You Strive for Self-Improvement?

I travel into Manhattan several times a week. On the train, I have forty-five minutes of quiet alone time. Since I am totally intimidated or should I say challenged by iPod, iPad technology and feel like a dinosaur, I enjoy my reading time. I tried reading with my Kindle, but I couldn't get the hang of underlining and folding pages like I do when reading a book. I like to do that so I can more readily use the books I read as reference material. I know there is a way to do it electronically, but I feel more comfortable doing it the old-school way. Lately, I have been listening to some incredible books on Audible.com.

I try to read (listen) about how to apply business principles to make myself a better person. I read about communication skills, leadership and self-help. I reread Napoleon Hill's Think and Grow Rich, (what I call my "business bible" and Yesterday for Today and Tomorrow principles I apply to my mentoring of young professionals. I try to learn about ways that I can be of better service to people around me so that, perhaps, I can help them to overcome some of the obstacles that I have been confronted with, in my business career.

I walk from Penn Station (Thirty-Third Street and Eighth Avenue) to Forty-Seventh and Sixth. I try to keep a brisk pace so that I get the best cardio workout to make use of the time. As I walk, I take the time to reflect on the things that are happening around me, and I reflect on what I can do to make myself a better person.

Have you ever played "If you step on a crack, you'll break your mother's back. If you step on a line, you'll break your mother's behind"? Speaking of integrity, would you want your mother's back to crack or would you want to protect your mother any way you could? I avoid the cracks and lines, just lamenting about my mom and how special she is to me. Somehow, it always fills my mind as I stride through the busy streets of the city.

When your children and parents both need care, where do your responsibilities lie? What are your responsibilities to your in-laws? What is the extent of your financial obligation to your parents? When there are multiple siblings, how should the fiduciary responsibility be delegated?

I enjoy walking, and somehow, I always look down as I walk. I constantly find coins all the time, which I save up. I have a couple of favorite street beggars, young adults who are severely handicapped, Willie and Sabrina. Whether I am having a good week in business or a difficult week, I always find a couple of dollars in my pocket to give them. No matter what, I am blessed and realize how much better off I am than they. There have been times when on my busy run to finish my errands and get back to Penn Station that I have passed by Willie and Sabrina, my mind somewhere else. I always double back to drop a couple of dollars in their cups and see the smile that it brings to their faces. You see, I have learned the importance of perhaps making whomever I can, that I touch, feel better about themselves and, perhaps, let them feel a little more important than they have ever felt before. I make it a point to learn the names of the people that clean my office building, the security guards, the delivery people, and all the service people that make my life easier. I try to show a genuine interest in who they are. I realize that, which cost me nothing, is a treasure to share by putting others in a role where they feel they matter. I am blessed in who I am, and I feel better about those I can touch. In turn, they touch me.

Tradgedy or A New Beginning

My dad semi-retired from our store in 1983, and now, I ran the family business. Every year, through my efforts, our store had been experiencing exponential growth. Unfortunately, our family owned retail store was robbed three times between 1986 and 1996, losing over $2,000,000 cumulatively due to these burglaries, and I could no longer sustain to be in business. Yes, I had insurance, but the first company went into receivership due to embezzlement, and after ten months of investigation, the second company discovered that one of my employees set up the hit and that voided the warranties of my policy so that they would not have to pay me. I could have filed for bankruptcy but decided that if I was going to remain in this business and keep my reputation clean, I needed to make arrangements with all of my suppliers and repay them for the merchandise. I wanted to be able to look in the mirror each morning and be proud of the person that I was. In 1998, I opened a new business, working from an office rather than a store.

I have over forty years of owning and running my own business and always thinking of myself as being successful where nobody ever told me how to run my business or how I could do it better.

With the need to build a new entity and create opportunities, I began to go to business networking meetings. Since 1998, I have been very involved in the Long Island business community and network. As a matter of fact, I have been called the icon of the community. I meet about three hundred to five hundred new people each year. I know about one thousand attorneys, eight hundred financial advisors, four hundred promotional products dealers, three hundred printers, etc. I guess you get the idea. The purpose of good networking is in creating relationships to further each other's business. The motto is Givers Get. Many of the eons of people I have come across call themselves coaches. Some of them are business coaches, and some of them call themselves life coaches. Some of them are certified in many areas, and some of them were just "consultants" that have years of experience working in their respective fields, either laid off or cannot find a job, found a way to use their practical experience to make an income. It sort of turns you off when people tell you how they can help you to change your life.

I attended a couple seminars to gain further knowledge and grasp on my business. One of them was a sample TAB (The Alternative Board) session, sponsored by a Long Island bank. Steve Davies, Facilitator and Partner of TAB, became my trusted advisor as I became a paid member for a couple of months. I sat through monthly TAB board meetings, weekly coaching sessions, and coaching calls. I gave in to the concept of being coached by a professional business coach, and I saw the value of being taught to work in my business instead of on my business.

TAB's board meetings put the power of collective wisdom, accountability, drive and creativity, and clarity of advice in your hands to align your business vision with your personal vision and ensure you get what you want out of life. I meet and share business expertise, solve business challenges, help each other seize new opportunities, and create actionable strategic plans, all under the guidance of a qualified facilitator (go to the TAB website).

I learned that my biggest problem was that I was constantly getting in my own way. I learned that I had issues with time management, and I needed to find someone to whom I could assign simple tasks to do so that I could free myself up to handle the important tasks of creating income.

I left TAB after three months because it wasn't as beneficial for me as it might have been for others.

I realized that the cost was overbearing, and I seemed to be offering more value to the other members of my board than the value I was receiving. My resolve was that I hired a bookkeeper, who came in twice a month, to handle paying bills, and I hired a part-time person to do simple data processing tasks, which took up a lot of my time.

* * *

My friend, Rakesh Bhargava was a facilitator of two Goal Cultivator communities that met quarterly to cultivate and harvest goals and participant's views of their futures. He facilitated PAC (Presidential Advisory Council) for CEO clubs in New York. He initiated an entrepreneurial study group of nine CEOs of small but growth-oriented companies with the sole aim to study how to grow member's income along with leisure time. Rakesh was a member of Dan Sullivan's elite CEO group. Dan Sullivan, from Montreal, is known as the strategic coach, and he has been coaching top-performing entrepreneurs for many years.

Rakesh asked me to join one of his communities. Through the Goal Cultivator Community, I met several associates who have impacted me that became close friends and trusted associates who have also become my mentors and inspirations (as I am to them) and have helped to take me and my business to new heights. Together, we continue to stay in touch and keep each other accountable.

* * *

Joe Nunziata, a long-time friend and mentor, who I frequently lunched with, is the author of several books, one of which is Karma Buster. He shows people a way to open their minds to unlimited possibilities. His enlightening book will give you a new definition of karma. You will also discover the keys to uncovering your karmic cycle and clearing the energy that is holding you back. In his previous book, Spiritual Selling, Joe talks about clearing your chakras. (chakras are centers of energy located on the midline of the body). In Joe's teachings, he shows new insights and valuable tools that will change the way you view sales and business. It combines spiritual principles with proven sales tactics. The result, the Attractor Sales System™, a system that will transform your business.

* * *

Karen Garvey, author, intuitive, speaker, friend, who in our initial meeting. We had seven coincidences that tied us together. I learned that there are no coincidences; everything happens for a reason, and Karen was put in my life for a reason. After obtaining her MBA, Karen acquired extensive business and writing experience, authoring/coauthoring many articles and books. She presently addresses audiences and appears in the media about reaching success, offering practical guidance for discovering one's path to fulfillment. Karen regularly connects with nonphysical sources of guidance to provide frequent insights into our earthly existence through enlightening essays for workshops, audio programs, and books. Her first book, The Answers (her answer to the Secret) contains the answers to your questions about life. Karen writes, *"There is a valid reason you feel lighter when you commune with nature; it is because you are temporarily removing your cloaks and touching upon your authentic self"* (go to www.KarenGarvey.com).

* * *

Marcy Neumann is a visionary who teaches people of all ages and genders how to hone their LOA success and achieve the manifestation success they are looking to enjoy. She is a published author, registered nurse, Reiki master teacher, ordained minister, certified hypnotherapist and spiritual healer. As the HeartShift coach and through her company, Heartlites Inc., Marcy assists people in the development of the wholeness of their being. Marcy has taken the "what now" question expressed by so many and created "right here, right now" tools for bringing it all together.

Marcy Neumann, creator of the Letting Go to Let In and the unique CELLpH (Self) Love™ programs teaches us to create the conscious awareness of how we are feeling at any given moment, appreciate its impact upon us and then drive us to the appropriate action pointed toward our ultimate goal of being happy, healthy, and whole. She is not only your mentor, guide, and coach but a student of her own teachings, as well as she, practices her own teachings each and every day. She was there, right where you are now, unsure of where to go, which way to turn to get out and once out, what to do to keep from falling back. That's what the Letting Go to Let In program is all about, starting with a shift in your heart and your frequency that ends with a shift in your life. Marcy is now known as The HeartShift coach.

* * *

Jerry Allocca is the president of CORE Interactive, author of Connected Culture, an Internet marketing authority, a speaker, and founder of CORE Interactive. I met him through our Goal Cultivator Community. In 2011, because of his accomplishments in digital marketing and his support of local businesses in furthering their marketing efforts, Jerry was awarded the Achievement in Digital Communications Award by the International Association of Business Communicators, Long Island Chapter, and today is the current President of IABC.

Teacher, mentor, award-winning digital marketer and entrepreneur, Jerry Allocca is a visible and vocal community member, using his skills to teach organizations of every variety how to succeed in our current economy and making an impact with his work every single day. He is a generous businessman and tireless networker. Today, Jerry is a frequent and much sought-after industry speaker on topics such as interactive marketing, social media, and website strategies. He has a passion for teaching and carries the intention of mobilizing community businesses and helping them make it through the difficult economic environment. Jerry is a close personal friend who has helped me immensely on several projects and bailed me out. We call one another on a continuous basis and enjoy our sushi lunches as we keep each other accountable for our forever-changing goals and actions. Although twenty years my junior, Jerry has been a great mentor, a driving force, and sounding board to whom I offer my thanks.

* * *

As you can see, through some of my networking and the people that I met and the experiences that I've had, I discovered, through understanding the law of attraction and that I also possessed a bit of clairvoyance and felt very connected to the Universe. I have been given a gift of seeing a purpose and understanding that even doing business had a greater purpose and that was to serve. Whether it is my community, my clients, my business associates or strangers, I learned to show gratitude first.

Are You Going to Tell Me What to Do?

It was in March 2011 that I started working one-on-one with my life and business coach, Pete Cracovaner, president of the Pinnacle Resource Group. I found Pete to be a very centered and spiritual teacher, which was the reason I felt that comfortable with him. Before that, I felt that nobody could tell me how to run my business, and who could be better than me? The way I hooked up with Pete was through a friend and business associate, Rob Basso, who owns and runs a very successful payroll company. Rob has expanded his resources and started several new ventures working with smaller, closely held businesses. "Basso on Business" was about helping small business and entrepreneurs like me build their businesses while tracking their progress. This was the precursor to being a part of a project that Rob pursued as he wrote his book The Everyday Entrepreneur, which is about the experiences of growing business in which he mentions the hardships small businesses experience and how there are ways to overcome those difficult times as long as one keeps a positive attitude.

Meanwhile, Rob Basso is an everyday entrepreneur with a mission, no, a passion for helping small businesses navigate their way to success. From the time he was in college, Rob has been involved in many business ventures, including an ice cream truck route in a highly competitive and contested area of Long Island. As the owner of the New York region's largest independent payroll processing firm, Advantage Payroll Services (www.liadvantage.com), he has interacted with thousands of business owners from virtually all business sectors. With over two thousand clients, he has his finger on the pulse of small business and has gained a wealth of knowledge about small business operations and growth. He is now sharing his insights with startup business owners, business executives, and entrepreneurs. Recently, he cofounded a national bank and has invested in multiple entertainment industry projects. By taking risks and developing creative concepts, he has built a reputation as a successful entrepreneur who is committed to assisting others seek and achieve their American dream.

Rob is the creator of BassoOnBusiness.com where he shares his experiences and those of other successful business people with a community of aspiring entrepreneurs. The community he has built is focused on inspiring the American entrepreneurial spirit. He has created a destination where business owners can get important tools, strategies, and real-world information that is vital to success.

Rob is the executive producer and host of a unique web business video program geared toward assisting small businesses in overcoming challenges. Each program is brought into the real world through Working Lunch with Rob, a monthly event where the new episodes of Basso on Business are premiered. The business owners and executives who attend offer their advice and solutions of their own. This empowers and motivates all attendees to implement positive changes in their organizations.

Rob is a respected small-business expert and sought-after speaker, who is regularly called upon by the regional and national media to comment on small business-related issues and trends. Rob is a frequent contributor on Fox News, Fox Business, and other national news programs. He has been interviewed by Entrepreneur and Time magazines and contributes blogs to American Express's OPEN Forum and the New York Enterprise Report. He is frequently interviewed by leading newspapers including Newsday, the New York Times, and Long Island Business News. He has appeared in national Associated Press, Forbes.com, MSN.com, and Bnet.com stories. He is also a frequent guest on radio programs across the nation and was recently a guest on the Sean Hannity Show.

Pete Cracovaner was Rob's personal coach at the time and offered to include me as a part of this process. The plan was that for a nominal fee, I would have ten private strategic coaching sessions with Pete and report my progress each week on a video flip camera. This video would be shown at a weekly luncheon promoting both my business and Rob's business along with the three other businessmen, who also participated in that process. The other business people who attended these luncheons could watch our progress and make comments about what they saw as progress versus detriment. Through this program, my business was promoted throughout the Long Island business community and was highlighted as part of the advertising process for the project. For me, it was a win-win situation.

One of the reasons I took part in this experiment was because I was faced with a situation that I was having trouble dealing with. My dilemma stemmed from a dream I had twenty-five years before, which never came to fruition. I had reconnected with this dream six years ago and could not understand why I had such a fabulous plan to launch products that everyone would want but could not get investors to participate in. Although everyone who I approached to invest with me said, "Wow! What a great idea. You'll make millions," nobody put their money where their mouth was. Prior to my contracting Rob and Pete, I had a discussion with Pete and told him about my frustrations. I shared what I thought to be a very detailed and thorough business plan, which I pitched to over sixty-five potential investors. Although all of them said it was going to be a very successful venture, none of them put their ink on the paper. I was having a difficult time trying to raise the funds that I needed to pursue my dreams.

Pete explained to me at our first preliminary meeting that either there was a problem with the marketing plan, the product, or the way that I was presenting the plan. His response was that the definition of insanity is that "if you do the same thing over and over again and get the same results, you need to change something." He told me that he thought he could help me as long as I would wholeheartedly dedicate myself to the process. I was sold on the opportunity and very excited that I was able to create a new roadmap in an attempt to accomplish something I had been dreaming about for twenty-five years and worked hard attempting to do for the past five–six years.

There comes a time when we're forced to choose between conflicting responsibilities or to make ethical compromises for good reasons. How do we decide what is right and, more importantly, what is right for us in our unique situation?

Would You Like to Advertise in the New York Mets Fan Appreciation Book?

In 1985, a salesperson came into my store and asked me if I wanted to advertise In the New York Mets fan appreciation book. Being a raving Mets fan, growing up in Queens, New York, I became very excited by the opportunity; however, my response to him was "Yes, however, I want to be the "Official Jeweler" of the New York Mets." He told me that he didn't know if that was possible, but his boss,

John F. was the owner of a company who instead of that did major promotions throughout seventeen of major league baseball stadiums. These promotions included Snapper Mowers, Pancho Day, and Swingline Staple Day.

At a meeting with John a couple of weeks later, I discussed my intent to design and sell baseball team logo jewelry. I developed a business plan and created prototype samples of rings, pendants, cufflinks, and key chains with the New York Mets logo. We figured with his contacts and my background, we would be able to create a profitable venture. John and I became close friends over the years, and we still are today. My general counsel, John F., and I sat through many meetings with William Shea and the New York Mets organization. I needed to hook up with Drew Sheiman, at that time the director of licensing for the NY Mets. Prior to 1986, all license agreements were made directly through each individual team.

A very good friend of mine was the salesperson for handled the WHN account. Adena and I drew up a contract for my new venture to advertise on WHN, the Mets TV, and radio station.

How excited was I when Adena called and told me on the Thursday afternoon prior to spring training that she made room for two more people to attend spring training for the 1986 season, all expenses paid. I asked if I could bring my son Michael, whose tenth birthday was in two days. Of course, she said yes. I went home that day and discussed the opportunity with Michael's mother and begged her to let him go with me. That night, we packed up our clothes, my prototypes of the Mets jewelry, and told my son about the journey we were about to embark upon. I had never seen this redheaded kid so excited. The following day, early Friday morning, Michael and I drove to the airport and met with the rest of the WHN crew. We were on our way.

My First Trip to Spring Training Camp (1986)

Once off the plane, we were grouped together with the rest of the NY Mets sponsors. It was so interesting and exciting to meet everyone who was connected with the NY Mets. I was thrilled to be part of that group. As I got to know the other sponsors, I proudly showed everyone my sterling silver prototypes of fine jewelry that I intended to sell to the fans. Among the people I encountered were the DeBlasi brothers from DeBlasi Chevrolet and Michael Kahn from Kahn's hot dogs. We met Bob Murphy, the Mets announcer, and several of the Mets players, including Rusty "Big Red" Staub. (That is a whole other story that my redheaded ten-year-old son Michael will never forget.) Everyone loved my NY Mets jewelry and wished me great success.

All weekend long, I was trying to locate and meet Drew Sheiman, Director of Licensing to discuss a licensing contract. I had never met him before, and I was told that he was the key to obtaining my license with the Mets.

Michael and I enjoyed meals with the entire group. We went to the exhibition games and sat in the first row behind the home plate. What a thrill.

Saturday night, we went to dinner at the St. Petersburg Yacht Club where Ray Knight (then third baseman for the Mets) and his wife Nancy Lopez (LPA champion), Rusty Staub, Tim Chochran, Sid "El Cid" Fernandez, and a few others. After dinner, Sid Fernandez came back to the hotel with the bunch of us. We all sat in our suite drinking beer and watching Scar Face with El Cid" the left-handed wonder. It was an interesting night.

Sunday night rolled around quickly. It was the last day that we were going to be in Port St. Lucie, and I had an epiphany. I realized that all weekend long I had been playing basketball with a guy named Shy. Who would have thunk it... Shy was Drew Sheiman.

On the plane home, Drew told me to come to his office in the morning and we would draw up a contract. He loved the concept and the products and said that he would make our deal happen. I couldn't have been more excited.

Monday morning rolled around. I picked up my morning coffee as I sat in my office, waiting for Drew's call. I picked up the paper, and as looked through the sports section of the Newsday, my heart fell on the floor. Much to my dismay, there was an article reporting that Peter Heuberoff, then Senior VP of Major League Baseball changed my game plan. The article stated that new regulations required from that point on, that all licensing for any Major League team would have to go through Rick White's office at MLBP.

I immediately called Drew's office to find out what this meant to our pending arrangement. He told me we couldn't set a deal, and it was out of his control; however, he would set up a meeting for me with Rick White's office.

Two weeks rolled around. My general counsel and I were excited as we strolled down Thirty-Fourth Street in Manhattan to MLB's offices. When we arrived, we sat in an elaborate waiting room filled with outrageous sports memorabilia that stem all the way back to Major League Baseball's inception. A few moments later, we were ushered into a conference room where we sat with one of MLB's attorneys. He told us that a deal could be set; however, I needed to put a large sum of money in escarole as a guarantee for MLB royalties. I looked at John and I must have turned red as a beet. I was a small business-man, and there was no way that I could have raised that much money.

To my great disappointment, I did not launch my company at that time. The Mets had an outstanding season and went on to win the World Series that year (1986). It was a year that we projected could have brought in about $3,000,000 in revenue.

It wasn't in the cards. The universe had dictated that it wasn't my time as I later learned.

Coaching with the Right Person Makes a Difference

So now it was March of 2011, and with great reluctance, I began to work with Pete Cracovaner, Life Coach, Pinnacle Resourse Group. A business and life coach, like any therapist, has to get down deep into the inner workings of their clients. It is important to develop a report and create a more conducive environment to work within. After a couple of discussions, the first exercise Pete asked me to do was to take an online personal development profile survey. This survey is pretty much an assessment of the balance of life, showing the personal life wheel and the professional life wheel. This first is about relationships to family; mental, ethics, and beliefs; and social, physical, financial, and mental outlooks. The latter is in regard to productivity, people skills, time management, and sales influencing skills.

After completing the survey and having analyzed the results, Pete and I met. The real purpose of that survey was to determine in which areas I was an introvert or extrovert.

I scored 6.8 out of 10 in a category where I felt I personally excelled, in the area of integrity. Wow! That was more than just disturbing to me. I was totally taken aback because, in business, I bend over backward to do the right thing all the time. I usually give more than

I promise. In my personal life, I would give the shirt off my back to help another. In my charitable life, I give more than I can afford to give because I overly sympathize with the pain that others suffer from.

I looked up at Pete and said, "Six point eight...Pete, is this test accurate? 6.8 is a failing score. I'm appalled...That's not me!

I always considered myself a 10 in this category."

Pete's response to me was, "Do you remember the story of George Washington? After George cut down the cherry tree his dad came out and asked, 'Who cut down the cherry tree?' George responded, 'I cannot tell a lie. I cut down the cherry tree.' The real question here is did George Washington have integrity? If so, why did he cut down the cherry tree?" Pete continued to explain that it's not just being honest or telling the truth that constitutes a high level of integrity. It goes much deeper. We continued on the topic, Was it a living tree, a dead tree? Was it his father's tree or a neighbor's tree? Was it no longer bearing fruit or flowers? There are so many factors that how can anyone judge what is ethical or not, whether there is a breach of character or if one does not show integrity in action. Integrity, as I had defined earlier, is a combination of many factors. It has gray areas too. People do not perceive things the same way, and people do not look at right and wrong the same way.

In a later chapter, I would like to tell you more about Pete and the special way he connected me to my inner self.

I went on a quest that very day after meeting with Pete to find out the meaning of integrity, looking for different interpretations.

Here's what occurred.

The following day after I met with Pete, I was crossing the street. In the middle of the road was a nail (about three inches in size). I thought, "What if a car ran over this nail? It could get a flat tire." And so I kicked the nail to the curb and walked the other way. As I did this, I thought to myself, "I really should pick up that nail and put it in the garbage. That would have been the difference between 6.8 and 10; however, at that time, I did not." About an hour later, after running errands in ten different offices, I felt something in the heel of my shoe. I thought that perhaps I stepped on a piece of jewelry or a piece of gum or a thumbtack. When I looked at the bottom of my shoe, I was beyond flabbergasted. There, driven straight into the heel of my shoe was a three-inch nail with only the head sticking out. My first thoughts were, "Na, it couldn't be." It takes a lot of pressure to drive a nail through the heel of your shoe. I would have really had to kick the nail with tremendous force to drive that nail, but I didn't. It couldn't be the same nail, could it?

It was as though there was a divine intervention, some message that was sent to me by a universal power. I removed it and put it in my attaché case. Shortly after, I went back to the original place where I kicked the nail, and it wasn't there. There are no coincidences. That afternoon when I arrived back at my office, I placed the nail in a jewelry box on the back of my credenza behind my desk, thinking, "There was a reason this nail was gifted to me. There was a purpose. The universe was telling me something, and in time, I would figure it out."

Here we are; it's more than a year. Much has happened since. I launched a business that was something I dreamt about for over twenty-five years. It was a huge undertaking, and everyone that heard about it also though it was a home run. Well, with many of the best people at my side, we commenced business and worked our butts off, invested beyond my capacity, and faced every unforeseen challenge only to close it down inside of six months due to being undercapitalized.

"The Nail of Integrity" has been staring me in the face all this time. Yes, there is a purpose. Byproducts can sometimes arise when you're not looking, and sometimes these byproducts can be more relevant than the original plan.

Integrity in Religion

*"It's not what we profess, but what we
practice, that gives us integrity."*
Sir Francis Bacon

"The integrity of faith is a matter of substance not show, influence not impressions, and influential actions not rhetorical declarations. The most profound obedience to God imaginable may take place in a silence as dense as that of a graveyard or as far from public view in personal expression.

Dr. Henry Cloud from his book Integrity: The Courage to Meet the Demands of Reality states: "All of the world's great religions praise integrity as a principal spiritual virtue. The Eight-Fold Path of Buddhism—that is right understanding, right thought, right speech, right action, right livelihood, right effort, right mindfulness, and right concentration—is nothing if not a complete guide to living with integrity in every sphere of life."

In 1831, Alexis de Tocqueville, French historian, visited America and wrote the following account:

> "As few as 50 years ago, we lived in a nation
> where a man's word was considered his bond, a

handshake sealed a transaction, and people took
pride in honest and upright behavior."

In March 1994, a USA Today-CNN-Gallup poll resulted in 69 percent responding that religion as a whole is losing its influence on
US life. While the polls tell us that forty million Americans attend
church at least four times a month, they also reveal that 86 percent
of the politicians, journalists, and media personnel infrequently or
never attend church. Thus the secularizing influences of our government, educational system, and entertainment industry have polluted
our nation. This secular triumph has left many Americans isolated,
confused, and alone.

By definition, the word "integrity" comes from the root word integer,
which means whole, complete, or entire. It is firm adherence to a
code of morals, values, and behavior.

By demonstration, integrity is uprightness of character, trustworthy
action, and responsible commitment.

By determination, integrity is a standard of incorruptibility—a
refusal to be false to a trust, responsibility, or pledge.

The bottom line is Christian integrity is a reality that sets the standard for the normal Christian life. Thus, integrity must be understood in the context of behavior.

Integrity is disciplined behavior.

Every day we make choices—what to do and how to live. Our lives
must reflect that we are governed by a code of absolutes that we will
not violate. This is the message of Joshua 24:15 and Ruth 1:16.

We are what we choose, and behavior is a result of choice. We make an intellectual-emotional- spiritual decision to function in a way that brings the highest productivity to our lives.

Integrity is determined behavior.

The key to integrity is to determine a sense of inner directedness that does not yield to the pressures of the age, that identifies with the highest rather than the lowest, the best rather that the worst, the ideal rather than the average, the excellent rather than the mediocre. It reaches for the deepest resources in Christ, stands up, and says, "I'm taking charge of my behavior. I'm not going to bend to the temptations and frustrations of the world." It says, "I know whom I have believed and am persuaded that He is able to keep what I have committed to Him until that Day" (2 Timothy 1:12 NKJV).

Integrity is demonstrated behavior.

Integrity is a lifestyle characterized by the indwelling of God's word. It means having one's act together and exemplifying the Christlike life in every circumstance. The apostle John put it this way, "But whoever keeps His word, truly the love of God is perfected in him. By this, we know that we are in Him. He who says he abides in Him ought himself also walk just as He walked."

Paul L. Walker, Ph.D., is senior pastor of Mount Paran Church of God, Atlanta, Georgia.

"1. Am I truthful? Are there any conditions under which I will tell a lie? Can I be depended on to tell the truth no matter what the cost?

"2. Am I honest? Can I be trusted in money matters? In my work, even when no one is looking? With other people's reputations? With myself or do I rationalize and become defensive?

"3. Am I pure? In my habit? In my thought life? In my motives? In my relations with the opposite sex?

"4. Am I selfish? In the demands I make on my family, spouse, or associates? Am I badly balanced, full of moods—cold today and warm tomorrow? Do I indulge in nerves that spoil my happiness and that of those around me? Am I unrestrained in my pleasures, the kind I enjoy without considering the effect…to take reasonable rest and exercise?

Am I unrestrained in small self-indulgences, letting myself become the slave of habits, however harmless they may appear to me?"

* * *

Many churches of all persuasions are hiring research agencies to poll neighborhoods, asking what kind of church they prefer. Then the local churches design themselves to fit the desires of the people. True faith in God that demands selflessness is being replaced by trendy religion that serves the selfish.
Billy Graham

As I pass temples and churches on Saturdays and Sundays, watching all the committed people entering or exiting their sanctuaries with their families, I can't help but to admire their commitment to their religious beliefs. I often ponder over the idea of what these people do once they return home from praying for peace and harmony, for solitude and promise. What do they do on the way home from church?

Do they "flip the bird" to someone who walks too slow so they can't get out of the parking lot fast enough? Do they take their children to play soccer and profess "run over that bastard" don't be afraid to knock him over and steal the ball, it's okay to trip the other guy... you're playing to win!

Do they profess integrity?

Søren Kierkegaard, a nineteenth-century Danish philosopher, theologian, poet, social critic, and religious author, who is widely considered to be the first existentialist philosopher writes:

> A person who has integrity is neither self-deceived nor self-divided. He or she tries to see themselves for who they are and isn't at war with themselves. Unfortunately, however, we humans are both self-deceived and self-divided, at least according to some of the great medieval philosophers. The root of our self-deception and our self-division, they argue, lie in original sin. Original sin is the propensity of human beings to commit acts of moral evil, a propensity for which God is not responsible. The effects of this condition extend both to our intellect and our will, with the result that we are both deceived and divided, not recognizing who we are and willing our own and others' evil. Since we are responsible for these effects, we are both self-deceived and self-divided, and so not people of integrity. However, through the grace of God, we can become people of integrity, if we sur-

render to God, allowing God to work faith in us, thereby allowing us to see ourselves aright, for only through faith can we have understanding, and recreating our will so that it is oriented to the good rather than evil; subsequently, God strengthens us so that we may become ever more integrated, intellectually and volitionally, until we achieve union with him in the afterlife. This then is the medieval story of our fall, justification, and sanctification understood as a story of integrity lost and integrity regained.

In his talk to the Japanese Young Men's Christian Association, Baha'i leader Abdu'l- Bahá said, "The real bond of integrity is religious in character, for religion indicates the oneness of the world of humanity. Religion serves the world of morality. Religion purifies the hearts. Religion impels men to achieve praiseworthy deeds. Religion becomes the cause of love in human hearts, for religion is a divine foundation, the foundation ever conducive to life. The teachings of God are the source of illumination to the people of the world. Religion is ever constructive, not destructive" ("The Real Bond of Integrity is Religious in Character" in The Promulgation of Universal Peace, October 7, 1912).

When I was a kid, we listened to our parents because we were told to. We respected our parents partly because they were our parents and partly because we were afraid not to. Call it respect or call it fear.

Growing up in a family whose greatest asset was being part of the family left a very large impact on me.

There was a very close relationship between my father and mother and my father's parents, his sisters and their families. I remember traveling to the Bronx, where my grandparents lived, to celebrate every Jewish holiday. My grandmother would cook the most outrageous meals and my grandfather would chant prayers. My immediate family, my aunts, uncles, and my cousins would just sit there. I remember how my mother dressed my brother and me in woolen dress pants and a white itchy starched shirt with a bow tie. The pants itched like hell and caused a rash, but I was told to be quiet not to cry or complain, so I never uttered a word. We all sat there out of respect to my grandparents.

I heard a funny story about a guy who was running late for one of the most important meetings of his life, and he can't find a parking space. He throws up his hands and says, "God, if you give me a spot, half of what I make from this deal I'll give to charity." Before the words escaped through his mouth, someone pulls out of a space that's right in front of him! He looks back up to the heavens and says, "Oh, never mind. I just found one!"

Short Story:

> Two men were fishing in a stream when they noticed that a nearby bridge was falling apart. Every time a vehicle would drive across it, another piece would fall and the entire bridge would shake dangerously. Finally, after a large truck passed over, the bridge completely fell apart in the middle. The two fishermen knew that if a car came around the bend, the driver would never know that the middle of the bridge was gone; the whole thing could come crashing

down, damaging the vehicle and injuring the driver. One of the men looked at his friend and said, "We've got to do something. What would be the Christian thing to do?"

His friend thought for a moment and replied, "Build a hospital.

The Integrity of Samuel

This following addition is not meant to steer one in any direction whether you are a believer in one God, a Universal God or Universal Spirit, many gods or no god at all. It was borrowed from Bible.com.

In light of this research, Israel's high regard for Samuel comes as no surprise. Samuel was a man who exuded integrity. Nowhere is this best illustrated than in 1 Samuel 12:1–4:

> Samuel said to all Israel, "I have listened to everything you said to me and have set a king over you. Now you have a king as your leader. As for me, I am old and gray, and my sons are here with you. I have been your leader from my youth until this day. Here I stand. Testify against me in the presence of the Lord and his anointed. Whose ox have I taken? Whose donkey have I taken? Whom have I cheated? Whom have I oppressed? From whose hand have I accepted a bribe to make me shut my eyes? If I have done any of these, I will make it right."

"You have not cheated or oppressed us," they replied. "You have not taken anything from anyone's hand."

During his farewell speech, after having led Israel for decades, Samuel promised to repay anything he had unjustly taken from anyone. What a promise! Even more impressive was the people's response. Not one person rose up to make a claim against Samuel.

Samuel's honesty and personal integrity permeated every area of his life. These two characteristics directed how he regarded his possessions, his business dealings and his treatment of those who were weaker than himself. Samuel held himself accountable to the people he led. He opened himself up to the scrutiny of everyone with whom he had ever had dealings. As a result of this practice, Samuel's leadership has become legendary as this story has been told and retold throughout the centuries.

People want to know that their leader can be trusted. They want to know that leaders will keep promises and follow through on commitments. Promises and commitments are significant, though, in our day of Machiavellian ethics, it seems that they have become optional. We often seem more concerned with convenience and performance. We give lip-service to the importance of character, but we have the idea that when things get tough, the rules can be changed and commitments and covenants may be discarded at will.

But the Bible makes clear just how important our covenants are. Throughout the Scriptures, God focuses on the fact that he is a God who makes and keeps his covenants, that he can be trusted (1 Chronicles 16:15; Psalm 105:8). God can be trusted because he is trustworthy. That's the point: it always comes down to the issue of character, not just words. Biblical integrity is not just doing the right thing; it's a matter of having the right heart and allowing the person you are on the inside to match the person you are on the outside. This is how God is. This is how his people should be.

Perhaps a good word to think of is "consistency." There must be consistency between what is inside and what is outside. God is totally consistent. His actions and behaviors always match his character and nature. And his goal for us is nothing less. Christ's objective for his disciples is to make us disciplined people. In the words of John Ortberg, "Disciplined people can do the right thing at the right time in the right way for the right reason." Just like God.

(Kenneth Boa, "Integrity," Bible.com, October 24, 2005, https://bible.org/seriespage/6-integrity)

Integrity and Ethics in Business

There is a natural alliance between the creation of wealth and the cultivation of character. Economic success is built on moral foundations—on the rule of law, faith, discipline, contracts, savings, integrity, a work ethic. Sound families that elevate these beliefs are the source of much of our culture's strength and future.
Jack Kemp

* * *

Do They Possess Integrity and Dis-integrity:

Business Responsibility Lessons from Islam by Dave Bamber

Dave Bamber is research coordinator at Liverpool Hope University Business School. He states the idea that managers ought to somehow promote organizational integrity is not a new one…It has, however, recently become an idea closer to the forefront of managerial concerns. Despite a considerable degree of imprecision, "managing for integrity" seems to reflect at least three interrelated assumptions.

1. Having integrity in some way contributes to the wholeness or completeness of a person and leads to consistency in thought and action over time.

2. This wholeness or completeness derives from having a defined and wholehearted interest in abiding by the right sorts of ethical principles and values. When conducting business, persons with integrity do not, so to speak, check their ethics at the door and also seek to meet ethical demands beyond mere compliance to the letter of the law.

3. Organizational integrity is assumed to be achieved by aligning and unifying individual, company, and societal ethics in ways that promote a positive ethical-organizational culture.

- Managers should understand and define socially acceptable ethical expectations, principles, and values. These expectations, principles, and values should be documented in company mission statements, policies, and procedures.
- Steps should be taken to bring ethical principles and values to bear in practice, which includes executive commitment and leadership, adequate resource allocation, communication and training, and positive and negative forms of motivation.
- Measurable objectives based on ethical principles and values should be established and progress made toward meeting objectives tracked. Companies ought to continually improve organizational ethical performance.
- Instances of unethical and/or illegal conduct and failures to meet defined objectives should be subject to some form of corrective and preventive action.

Additionally, larger and more influential companies should seek to export similar integrity based programs down their supply chains and even across their industry. Collectively, these sorts of suggestions seem to reflect a process and quality oriented style of organizational management. While very sympathetic to quality and process oriented management principles, they criticized the limitations of these principles and associated methods when applied to understanding the role of integrity in organizational-ethical management.

Those of you who work in large business climates, what is it that you expect from your bosses and your business associates?

Any management seminar will teach that managers have to do with they say they're going to do. Whether they promised reward for good work or punishment for bad, they must deliver. If they do not, they will lose the respect of their coworkers. "Integrity is the basis of trust," writes Warren Bennis, "which is not as much as an ingredient of leadership as it is a product." In other words, a reputation for integrity, which one must possess in order to be trusted by colleagues, must be earned. Integrity in turn creates the trust that we need for ordinary social and political intercourse.

* * *

Giving Up? Not an Option

In 1983, 1991, and in 1993, our family business of almost forty years was burglarized and robbed. Each time, the stress nearly killed us, but my parents always instilled in me the ability to show countenance and strength in every situation I faced. We dug in the trenches and worked our way out. It wasn't easy, but giving up was not an option. Client's jewelry, vendors' merchandise, and our own jewelry were stolen. We lost hundreds of thousands of dollars' worth of goods. We had insurance, but we were insured by a surplus lines insurance carrier which means it was an out of New York State insurance company. Our brokers recommended we go this way because the premiums were less expensive, but what we didn't realize was that if the insurance carrier became insolvent, we would not get paid. Who would ever think an insurance company would go belly up? Well, ours did.

We learned that if you have a New York State carrier and they go bust, the New York State solvency department would cover the loss.

I guess we weren't so smart.

My dear friend Adrian Miller, Sales Trainer and Author of the Blatant Truth: 50 Ways to Sales Success, wrote an article that resonates with me:

> Most of us were raised with the idea that giving up was something to be avoided, that persistence, hard work and tenacity were what was needed to be successful. Why I can hear my mom now as I struggled through my math homework as she readied dinner.
>
> "Don't give up. If you try harder you'll be able to get it." I wish that I could report that she was right and that by simply trying harder and not giving up I had my eureka moment, and I got it. It didn't really happen. I sucked at math and struggled my way through it for all of my school years.

My failure at math notwithstanding, as a pretty competitive and somewhat driven person I can't much say that I like the idea of giving up. I too believe that tenacity is a terrific attribute and stick-to-it-tiveness is truly admirable.

Giving up? Haha, never.

But is that really the best solution? Not really because sometimes giving up is simply what should be done. You've given it your sales best, and the prospect is still recalcitrant, not giving an inch, and every additional moment spent wooing and attempting to win this prospect is costing you time and money.

You've worked with this client for years, but they've changed models and have started down a path that is not in sync with your desired corporate direction. You've trained, coached, incentivized, and motivated and your employee is still not able to perform at a satisfactory level. And that's just for starters. Yes, there are many situations, in which, giving up is the sensible, honorable and most satisfactory solution. This doesn't mean you have to shed your sense of persistence; it merely provides you with another option to which you can turn when there is nothing left to be done.

As I have mentioned earlier in this book, I come from a family retail jewelry business which evolved from a gift store to a full-fledged fine jewelry store through the hard work and perseverance of my parents and me. We were burglarized many times, but through countenance and determination to succeed, we endured for forty years and never quit.

Where is the Integrity? Manufactures have Become Profit Centers and Lack Commitment to the Consumer

These days manufacturers, distributors and retailers have become so ingrained in creating profits rather than making a commitment to the consumer. Advertising has become so deceptive. If a potential buyer believes that the claims of the manufacturer are true, where lies the liability for false advertising when the product does not deliver what it claims to do?

So many of the commercials we see have little to do with the product being presented. They are mere attention grabbers. The larger the event i.e. Super Bowl, World Series, Olympics, the more sublime the advertising has become. The ads are meant to capture peoples emotions so the consumer identifies with the characters or situations and not so much with the product or it's usage. As I sit and watch television, from time to time I ask my wife "What was the commercial selling?"

We should be a "grateful society" and thankful for what we have. Commercials are meant to make us feel as though we are deficient in so many areas that we need more to satisfy our psyche's. We have become a society of instant gratification due to the efforts of the advertisers.

We are constantly exposed to pictures of starving children and animals who are suffering from abuse or poverty. These ads and commercials, letters and donation envelopes mailed to us from not-for-profit organizations appeal to our senses and make us feel guilty.

There are many companies which, upon seeing the success of a product, may piggyback on an idea to come up with a similar product. The savvy consumer will shop around for a more durable alternative.

When companies produce products to be more competitive in the marketplace, there is the risk we take as consumers to purchase products that do not last as long.

Every time I see a commercial for a drug on TV, I laugh.

Then, there are the drug companies who have great remedies for every ailment and illness. A pill that cost three cents to produce costs $56.00 to the consumer. Yes, there is costly research and development, but we have to consider the circumstances as well. So you have severe headaches. Would you rather have the pain from a headache or take XYZ medication, which may cause serious side effects including the following:

- Heart attack and other heart problems.
- Injury during a magnetic resonance imaging (MRI). The XYZ contains metal parts and must be removed before an MRI.

- Allergic contact dermatitis (ACD). Some people have had a serious skin reaction called ACD where XYZ is applied. Symptoms of ACD include skin itching, redness, irritation, blistering, peeling, or tenderness. You should stop using XYZ and call your healthcare provider if you have any of the symptoms of ACD. If you have or have had ACD while using XYZ and need to take ABC by mouth or injection, your first dose of ABC should be given in your healthcare provider's office or in another medical setting.
- Changes in color or sensation in your fingers and toes (Raynaud's syndrome).
- Stomach and intestinal problems (gastrointestinal and colonic ischemic events). • Problems with blood circulation to your legs and feet (peripheral vascular ischemia).
- Medication-overuse headaches. Some people who use too many XYZ may have worse headaches (medication overuse headache).
- Serotonin syndrome is a rare but serious problem that can happen in people using XYZ, especially if XYZ is used with anti-depressant medicines called SSRIs or SNRIs.

Ask your healthcare provider or pharmacist for a list of these medicines if you are not sure. Call your healthcare provider right away if you have any of the following symptoms of serotonin syndrome: mental changes such as seeing things that are not there (hallucinations), agitation, or coma; fast heartbeat; changes in blood pressure; high body temperature; tight muscles; trouble walking; or nausea, vomiting, or diarrhea.

- Increases in blood pressure. You should not use XYZ if you have uncontrolled high blood pressure.

- Serious allergic reactions. Get medical help right away if you have any of these symptoms of a serious allergic reaction: swelling of your face, lips, mouth, or tongue; trouble breathing; wheezing; severe itching; skin rash, redness, or swelling; dizziness or fainting; fast heartbeat or pounding in your chest (tachycardia); or sweating.
- Seizures. Seizures have happened in people taking sumatriptan who have never had seizures before. Talk with your healthcare provider about your chance of having seizures while you take XYZ. The most common side effects of XYZ include pain, tingling, itching, warmth, discomfort, or a change in the skin color at the application site of XYZ. Most people have some skin redness after removal of XYZ. This redness will usually go away in twenty-four hours. Tell your healthcare provider if you have any side effect that bothers you or that does not go away. These are not all the possible side effects of XYZ. For more information, ask your healthcare provider or pharmacist.

So do you take this drug or just shoot yourself?

Deceptive advertising and Social Proof

As I will take up in later chapters, advertisers love to inform us of when a product is the fastest growing or largest selling because they don't have to convince us directly that the product is good; they need only say that many others think so, which seems proof enough.

The principle of social proof states that one important means that people use to decide, or what to believe or how to act in a situation is to look at what other people believe or are doing there.

The principle of social proof can be used to stimulate a person's compliance with a request by informing the person that many other individuals are, or have, been complying with it. Social proof is most influential under two conditions. The first is uncertainty. When people are unsure when the situation is ambiguous, they are more likely to attend to the actions of others and to accept those actions as correct. In ambiguous situations, for instance, the decisions of bystanders to help are much more influenced by the actions of other bystanders then when the situation is a clear-cut emergency. The second condition under which the social proofs most influential is similarity: People are more inclined to follow the lead of similar others."

Called the Egregious Breach of Integrity?

Dr. Oz, medical doctor and TV personality, who has been an advocate of holistic means for promoting health and wellbeing, was under attack.

In an article by Mike Adams, the Health Ranger, titled "Mainstream media Fail: Sleazebag doctors attacking Doctor Oz have histories of criminal fraud and ties to Monsanto's 'Discredit Bureau,'" he writes:

> The mainstream media has just been suckered by the "Monsanto Discredit Bureau" into glyphosate or GMOs. With some notable exceptions, most mainstream media outlets operating today are now functioning as Monsanto propaganda mouthpieces, viciously attacking those who should be celebrated as true American heroes.

To achieve their latest defamation campaign against Doctor Oz, the mainstream media relied on a fraudulent and slanderous letter signed by ten doctors addressing Columbia University, demanding Dr. Oz resign from a senior staff position there. But in reporting this, the entire mainstream media failed to look into the backgrounds of the doctors signing the letter. If they had done any background research at all, they would have found some astonishing things that completely discredit the letter and the malicious, contrived attack on Oz...

> What we have with all this is a monumental failure of journalism -- mainstream media outright rejects the very idea that they should look into the 10 doctors making these allegations against Oz. In their rush to attack Doctor Oz, or the Food Babe, or the Seralini science team, mainstream media publishers utterly fail to see how they are being manipulated by the Monsanto Discredit Bureau. Or, alternatively, they are obedient to it and just following orders.

Challenges of Employee Theft

Companies, large and small, face many challenges; the greatest is from employee theft. Time is the number one issue. Whether it is from employee texting, personal e-mailing on company time, cigarette breaks, extended lunch or coffee breaks—these are all about employees stealing time.

Several surveys have been taken; whereas, it has been found that the average smoker, who smokes one pack of cigarettes alone, takes four hours of cigarette breaks each week. What this equates to is that the simple impact of this is quite astounding:

1. Loss of productivity.
2. Resentment of peers who have to make up for time lost by their fellow workers.
3. Medical ramifications of illness due to smoking and illness due to secondhand smoke.

Many employees and entrepreneurs, as well, take the liberty of going beyond the corporate threshold. In other words, they take liberties that are not given.

> Employee theft also includes taking paper clips, copy paper, and other office supplies home. At

what point does any of this become employee theft? Certainly, these things are not as severe as writing ghost checks to an employee that doesn't exist, however, at what point do we call this theft? These are other forms of employee theft:

- Embezzlement, for instance, can devastate small businesses, wrecking owners' personal and business finances at the same time. Forgery of company checks for personal gain.
- Using a ghost payroll, which occurs when one or more employees create "phantom" employees, submit time cards for those employees, and then cash their paychecks themselves.
- Theft of raw materials or inventory items.
- Outright theft of cash from a register drawer sweethearting." This term refers to an unethical practice wherein an employee will grant a friend or another person a discount at the register or ring up fewer items than the person has actually bought.

1. Theft of information. Internal theft of information has become an increasingly serious problem for employers, especially since huge amounts of meaningful information are commonly stored in computer

files. In fact, security consultants point out that employees often are more computer literate than their bosses, which may strengthen the temptation to abscond with proprietary information or otherwise engage in illicit activities.

2. An employee may be stealing include missing records (such as shipping and receiving bills).

3. Company checks that bounce, customer complaints about missing or late deliveries, hefty payments made for "miscellaneous" purposes in employee expense claims, and managers who insist on performing clerical duties.

Stealing from the Jobsite: Petty versus Huge Employee Theft

Why do employees steal from their workplace? by Matt Keating, The Guardian, October 7, 2005,

> Although the report found only a small number of staff to be responsible, there are concerns that employee theft and fraud is more widespread than it might appear. "Most people who steal from work - whether time theft, fraud, embezzlement or theft of goods or products - are not doing so because they are professional thieves or dishonest people," says Terry Shulman, author of Biting The Hand That Feeds: The Employee Theft Epidemic. "They slip into it a little at a time, mostly out of a combination of disgruntlement and compulsion."

Shulman says most employees who steal from work are honest in other areas. "But for most there is a sense of entitlement and they don't think they are hurting anyone. Many feel angry and entitled to steal from work because of perceived feelings of being victimized or not being appreciated."

It is the nature of the working relationship that can provoke some employees to take advantage, particularly through deception. "You are much more likely to see this behavior where trust has broken down completely and people feel they are not being treated fairly. From an employee's perspective, they will justify it by saying 'I work extremely hard, yet get paid less than my peers'."

Workers who feel disengaged may be tempted to find their own compensations. "Theft should not be tolerated, but the odd personal phone call, for example, should be considered reasonable." Jo Causon from the Chartered Management Institute says a positive work environment from the start will help. "The employer needs to demonstrate the values of the organization and look to attract employees that share those values," she says. "Yet where there are incidents of theft or fraud at work, practical steps, such as changing locks and computer passwords and doubling inventory checks, need to be taken."

* * *

The US Chamber of Commerce estimates that 75 percent of all employees steal at least once and that half of these steal repeatedly. The chamber also reports that one of every three business failures is the direct result of employee theft. According to the US Department of Commerce, employee dishonesty costs American business in excess of $50,000,000,000 annually. It can happen in your company. How much does employee theft cost employers?

Reasons for Employee Theft

Perhaps the single biggest factor here is whether or not the employee has a problem with drug abuse. Many drug users hold legitimate jobs and a substantial number either deal or steal.

Some studies also show that employees who plan on quitting their jobs are much more likely to engage in stealing than are those who have no plans to leave. Characteristics of employees who steal include the following: they are more likely to harbor complaints, whether legitimate or illegitimate, about their employer.

Some employees steal simply because they know they can get away with it and won't get caught.

Morale and Trust

When employees themselves begin stealing from their employers, trust between coworkers is undermined and employee morale suffers. Employers who can't trust their employees have difficulty in delegating tasks, building teamwork, and creating a positive business environment.

Would You Buy Jewelry from a Used Car Salesman?

It's kind of ironic; however, I was just about finished editing this book when I realized that although I, being employed in the jewelry business for over forty-five years, didn't even think about writing a chapter about the integrity or lack of, in my industry.

The things I have seen and experienced can fill a book by itself. I have been dealing on Forty-Seventh Street in Manhattan, New York City, in the Diamond District, most of my business life. I have seen the street go from predominantly Hasidic Jews to Korean to Russian and Albanian to Turkish and Syrian to Columbian and other ethnicities. The moral standards throughout the industry have changed over the years. There was a time when a handshake meant your word. Today, you need to leave your' first born child for collateral, when you take merchandise from a vendor. In fact, so many people (vendors) owe each other money from trying to flip merchandise quickly to make a fast buck, that nobody trusts anyone anymore.

Although the diamond business became very scientific, and now that trading is based on certified stones, there are so many ways to dupe someone who doesn't really know the business. The business has become all about making money and not about treating the client with the proper respect. There is little integrity and lots of dishonesty.

As a consumer, if you don't have the proper education (which I offer my clients until they understand what they are buying and why they are paying whatever they are spending), there is much to know that affects price. You should always buy diamonds and jewelry from an establishment that you trust. Although you can obtain a good basic knowledge from the internet, you need a qualified professional who is willing to spend the appropriate time explaining what you need to know.

If you try to sell something on the street (Forty-Seventh Street in New York City's Diamond District or at any pawnshop, "cash for gold" dealer), instead of telling you what they would give you for an item, they ask you how much you want and then counter with an offer that might be insulting to some and taken only by fools. Some people sell because they get intimidated and others because they are needy and don't know the difference.

In 2008, when the banks were in trouble and many mortgage brokers were being put out of business, they found a new source of income. There was an influx of "cash for gold" stores, Internet offers, television advertising telling listeners to "put your unwanted gold in an envelope and send it to us and we will pay you the best price." In effect, the cost of running a store, advertising on television, isn't cheap. Who do you think paid the overhead expenses of these businesses? Mortgage brokers and others jumped on the bandwagon and began to sponsor "gold buying" parties. The offer generally was to pay the hostess $150 for groceries and $20 for every person who sold gold. When all was said and done, sellers were paid somewhere in the neighborhood of twenty cents on a dollar in cash. The people that were selling had no idea of the value of the gold they had. All they knew was that they were getting paid in cash and had extra spending money in their hands that they didn't have before. There are strict regulations that are upheld in most states, counties for any-one who buys gold. Buyers are required to be registered as a sec-ond-hand dealer and post a bond. Second-hand dealers are required to report (make a list) of all items that they purchase with the county police departments for the identification of potentially stolen arti-cles. This frenzy of gold parties became so prominent and was not properly regulated. Businesses were not recording the items and were not declaring income. When I did gold parties (to purchase gold), I always made a listing and paid by check. On one occasion, I recall that I sorted through and weighed the articles of one of the ladies at a party. She told me her husband thought she was crazy to sell her jewelry. I told her I could pay her $1,077 for her items. She looked at me in a very perturbed manner and said, "You're kidding me!" I asked, "Ma'am, is there anything wrong?" She told me that she sold twice as much stuff at a party a month ago and only got $200 cash.

Where was the integrity?

On the other hand, when was the last time you bought a car?

Do you know how salespeople are trained to sell cars?

Not just liars but devised tactics give them the upper hand. The thing about car dealers is they seem to like to keep you waiting.

It is important for the salespeople to feel they are controlling the customer. If you are waiting for them, they are controlling you. This obsession with control extended to job applicants too.

Here's how it works: When you negotiate, on the opening sheet, you have the customer's name and information on the top of the page (bold) along with the sticker price of the car they looked at. The sheet should be covered with numbers. It should be like a battle-ground. And management instructs their salespeople that they don't want to see the price dropping five hundred dollars at a pop.

Come down slowly, slowly, that is, the process begins by asking the customer how much they want for a monthly payment. Usually, the customer will say, "About $300." Then you just say, "Three hundred dollars up to?" And they'll say, "Well, $350." Now they've just bumped themselves $50 a month. That's huge. You then fill in $350 under the monthly payment box. You could use the "up to" trick with the down payment too. If Mr. Customer says he wants to put down $2000, you to say, "Up to?" And he'll probably bump himself up to $2,500."

You have to break them inside, make them understand that if they want our beautiful new car, they're going to have to pay for it.

A veteran car salesman said, "Thumb to thumb. Pump one, two, three, and out." Another vet says, "to combine the handshake with a slight pulling motion. This is the beginning of your control over the customer. This would prepare the up to be moved into the dealership where the negotiation would begin. The car lot handshake is some-times combined with the confident demand, "Follow me!" If you employ this method, you turn and begin walking into the dealership.

Car salesmen and women seem to exist in their own world. What they think is cool is viewed by the public as tacky and obvious. For example, why do they insist on wearing white shirts and silk ties? Or what about gold watches, rings, and chains? Who wears that stuff anymore? Don't they realize they are turning themselves into walking clichés?

So where do we go from here?

Wherein does the integrity lie?

Is it a game of how to overcome the customer and not to care about them but to maximize the bottom line. How often will a used car dealership see the same client?

Vacations... Beware of Vacation Scams

Has this ever happened to you?

So here we are in Puerto Plata in the Dominican Republic, a gorgeous hideaway in the Caribbean. The free transport to our hotel was a nice touch, a little crowded, and forty-five minutes of sniffing fumes instead of the twenty-five we were told. The ride was a bit uncomfortable and slow as we drove through the Puerto Plata city traffic. It seemed as though we arrived during rush hour. It was 5:30 p.m. It was very evident, as we drove through the countryside, it was obviously screaming of poverty. We were wondering what kind of accommodations we were going to find. We traded in a one-bedroom from our timeshare in Kissimmee, Florida, and had no idea what we were going to get in exchange. To our surprise, when we got to the hotel and checked in, we were told that our accommodations were upgraded to the presidential suites. It appeared to be a gorgeous resort in the middle of a severely poverty-stricken country. Our accommodations were way beyond expectations. The greeting and customer service offered a warm welcoming. Our first dinner was a white-glove restaurant, good food, plenty of wine, and excellent service. And we dined with another couple who also never visited that resort before. The bar service was great and all inclusive; therefore, drinks were free, so we hung out and drank after dinner, until midnight. On Sunday, we got up. got ready for the beach, but stopped to have breakfast at the VIP café. Once again the service was impeccable and the omelets and other food were wonderful. Understand now, this resort has seven beaches, twenty-seven bars, twenty-two restaurants, and lots of amenities. The first day, we went to one of the beaches where we were told it was for members only. A bit taken aback, but we went to an adjacent beach. At 9:30 a.m., there were few lounges left far from the entrance and the restaurant. The beach was overcrowded, and although there was cocktail service, the service was slightly mediocre. My wife and I left this beach and spent the balance of the day at the pool by our room. There were waterfalls and cabanas and lounges in the pool as well. It was truly beautiful. You would think that you could not want for more. Following a very pleasant evening, that night, we awoke to a gorgeous sunrise. We got ourselves ready and went for breakfast. We had great omelets, breads, and fruit. After breakfast, we were approach by what I call the hookers to bring us to a place where we could take a tour of the property. Jamison drove us to the "tower" where we met Juan Pablo, our tour guide (salesperson). We sat with Juan Pablo and talked as he asked us questions. One of them was about our two timeshares. We told him we might be interested in purchasing something only if we were able to trade them in, and he confirmed that if we were to purchase there, the company would give us the value of our timeshares in trade. He was a very pleasant guide who showed us all of the VIP amenities such as the VIP beaches and the VIP bars. We were told that if we became owners, we would be VIP members, entitled to all of these venues. He took us to the penthouses, the seven- bedroom villa on top of the cliff and overlooking the crescent bay below. It had an infinity pool, barbecue areas, living rooms upstairs and down. It was like something that you only see in travel brochures. We stopped at the oyster bar at one of the VIP beaches, the VIP wine bar at another area, and another bar at another VIP beach. We were truly wined and dined for about four hours. It was a great tour, and the properties are beautiful. We observed that there was also a lot of building and expansion going on throughout the resort. After the tour, we went back to the sales center where Juan Pablo introduced us to Noel, the senior sales coordinator, who asked us how much we liked the property and if we would like to be owners. That was where the negotiation began. We were asked how much available credit we had available on our credit cards. We both looked at each other and in unison said, "Not much." Noel and Juan Pablo left the table and came back a few minutes later with a spreadsheet of numbers. I guess they discussed our adventure and what kind of threshold Juan Pablo was able to detect. To make a long story short, we were given a number to buy into the vacation club ownership with a generous offering for out timeshares and credit for our present vacation week. Janise and I were very interested, and so I began to negotiate the price and the terms. At the entry level, we were going to get all the amenities as any other VIP vacation club member without the use of a golf cart. We came to terms after about an hour, and we were promised the use of the golf cart anytime we booked a vacation. At first Noel told us that it would cost us $1,000 extra. I refused. Then he said how about $560, and I refused, so he finally said, "Okay, I will include it at no additional cost." After we were rushed to sign all the contract pages, Janise and I left with a great feeling. We were getting rid of our timeshare maintenance of $2,100 annually and picking up a vacation club with unlimited weeks based on availability for our family and us with no maintenance fees. We had a four-day rescind period to cancel the deal, which gave us some comfort.

That night, of course, I read the contract thoroughly to find that although everything seemed okay, the golf cart was not included in our contract.

The following morning, after breakfast, I was back at the sales center and sat with the customer service manager to correct this dilemma. He told me that at the level we purchased, a golf cart is never included. We asked him point blank, "Where is the integrity of your sales team?" I explained my negotiation with Noel, and he said he would look into it and speak with management and get back to me by the end of the day, which he did. "Golf carts were only reserved for members at the next level of membership," he said. I told him that that might be a deal breaker and set an appointment for the following morning to speak with him. That opened a can of worms.

We spent the rest of the day speaking with other members, finding out what their disappointments were, and what options we had.

The following morning, we returned to the customer service center, and we were seated in a small conference room. I noticed a camera on the wall and nudged Janise as we both said, "Boy, would I like a copy of this tape" to the camera. After reiterating the events of the previous day and the terms that were discussed during our closing sales presentation, we shared the disappointments that we heard from other vacation club members and of promises made that were not kept. At this time, I told the customer service manager that we wanted to kill the deal. He turned red in the face and told us that that was okay; however, we were responsible for certain charges incurred because we were given VIP privileges for the past few days. As he excused himself and stormed out of the meeting, he returned about twenty minutes later with a bill for $4,700. My wife and I looked at each other and laughed. It had become more of a farce.

He clearly saw that there was no way that we were falling for that, and he changed his tune to appease us. Once again, my wife stated that the company was lacking in integrity and requested as part of our arrangement to remain members, she wanted a report filed against Noel and demanded that she receive a copy of the reprimand. The customer service manager agreed to do so. Hopefully, we will get what was promised as time goes on. Be wary and know what you're getting into before you leap. You're on vacation, and they get you in a soft spot and take advantage of your relaxed manner.

* * *

Public confidence in the integrity of the Government is indispensable to faith in democracy; and when we lose faith in the system, we have lost faith in everything we fight and spend for. Adlai E. Stevenson

Integrity in Government?

Remember that integrity is a conscious choice of an individual or organization to consistently act according to applicable rules and regulations, norms, culture, values, and ethical standards regulated by law and society's values.

Taken from the 2001–2009 Archive for the US Department of State:

> In the American experience, accountability of public officials is deeply ingrained within the Constitutional framework of the country. The political and civic culture of the United States is based on the notion that public officials should always perform their duties in the public interest. For example, the Constitution begins with the words "We the People." These words signify that all Government authority, whether exercised by elected or appointed officials, is ultimately derived from, and accountable to, the American people. Given this conception of public service, misconduct on the part of public officials presents one of the greatest threats to citizen confidence in the Government…

While the ethics program in the United States is designed to foster ethical conduct within Government, its ultimate goal is to maintain public confidence that Government is serving the interests, needs, and demands of all citizens. The structure of the program is only one model for achieving the challenging task of integrating accountability with democratic governance. It is designed to provide alternatives to relying strictly on law enforcement efforts to address wrongdoing by emphasizing prevention approaches that both complement and enhance law enforcement efforts. Over the years, this structure has proven effective in accounting for the size, extent, and diversity of the executive branch, while implementing systems of prevention, such as a code of conduct and financial disclosure. These elements are only a piece, albeit an important one, of the larger mission, to prevent conflicts of interest and provide the public with the access and information it needs to hold Government accountable to the highest standards of integrity and honesty. Ultimately we must reach for the standard Woodrow Wilson set in his classic work on democracy:

A sense of highest responsibility, a dignifying and elevating sense of being trusted, together with a consciousness of being in an official station so conspicuous that no faithful discharge of duty can go unacknowledged and unrewarded, and no breach of trust undiscovered and unpunished,—these are the influences, the only influences, which foster practical, energetic, and trustworthy statesmanship. (Amy Comstock, "Maintaining Government Integrity: The Perspective of US Office of Government Ethics," US Department of State Archive, May 29, 2001, http://2001- 2009.state.gov/p/inl/rls/rm/may/3403.htm)

* * *

It seems to me that we have a great breach in the ethics of many of our elected officials, who are working on their own personal agendas. I will leave you to your own opinions only because the intent here is not to get involved in political motives.

Election Day recently passed. I have never seen so much bombast in an attempt to discredit the other parties to the point at which I turned off every political commercial and commentary that did not discuss the real issues.

We hear news about the economy, healthcare, taxes, and immigration law. How does it affect us? We are all given a right and an obligation to research the issues confronting us in the decisions our government may be making. It may be our constitutional right and choice to vote, but how many people complain about what's going on and don't vote. They are the biggest complainers, and yet, they feel that their one vote is not going to make a difference.

You know what I have to say to these people? "Shut up and keep it to yourself!"

Where is your integrity when you are given a right and you refuse to exercise it?

Excerpts from an article, "Integrity in Government," written by Lloyd Weinreb for the 2003 Fordham Law Review

> Others have direct experience with the problems of promoting integrity in government and policing its lapses. I shall leave that difficult subject to them. I want to make some comments about what we mean by integrity in the context of government and to suggest that the circumstances of governance today weaken its meaning. Few disagree that integrity is one of the qualities most to be valued in public officials. We use the notion of integrity expansively as a general, all-purpose yardstick against which to measure public conduct. Yet it is an elusive concept, especially in relation to government and government officials.

If we want to make integrity a virtue, we should not set the standard so high that it is unattainable as a practical matter. In other words, integrity requires that government should not conceal or dissemble simply in order to secure the citizens' approval or to avoid their disapproval on what it does.

Crossing the Street

Does it affect our level of integrity when we cross at the corner of an intersection or crosswalk or the middle of the street? Can we cross wherever we want to?

The law says that pedestrians should always cross at the corner. Back in the '50s and '60s, I remember that there was an ordinance to prevent people from randomly crossing the street. At that time, police officers were giving tickets to people for jaywalking. What is jaywalking? It's simply crossing the street at the middle and not at the corner ends. I do that often as a result of my trying to keep a certain pace. If there is no traffic and the oncoming light is not in my favor, I don't think twice about crossing the street. When there is a red light and I come to a corner, do I stand there, waiting for the light to change when no cars are coming? No way!

Does this mean, in any manner that I lack integrity or does it lower my score?

Yeah. I am going against "society's rules," am I not?

While discussing this with my good friend Ron Tucker, he conveyed a story to me about an experience he had in Hong Kong. He approached a corner in the city of Hong Kong where the light was red and the No Walk sign was posted. As Ron put it, there were no vehicles in sight for miles. There was an Oriental gentleman walking next to him, who proceeded to cross the street against the light. As they both finished crossing, they were apprehended by two police officers. It seems that the fine in Hong Kong for crossing against the No Walk sign is $2,000 and fourteen days in jail. Oh my! Ron, who is a gentle soul and good talker and also being a vacationer in a new land, was able to talk his way clear. Unfortunately, for the other guy, Ron saw the police take him away.

Driving with Integrity

How many times have you nearly been blindsighted by someone that refuses to stop at a stop sign?

It is especially important when we are driving with young kids or adolescents in our car to drive safely and prudently when it comes to obeying road signs and speed limits, after all, they will soon be on the road themselves?

We need to set an example. I like to say, "Drive with integrity." I can never forget the lesson I learned when driving with my son as he was learning to drive. As I drive through my suburban neighborhood, I constantly see people drive right through stop signs. Most people don't even slow down to acknowledge that the sign does exist. I've noticed that some do. Sometimes, they slow down and pause just enough so that when you (who do not have a sign) are turning, they cut you off and look at you as though it was your fault.

The other night as I was driving through the neighborhood, a car flew through a stop sign without even slowing down. So as a concerned citizen, I flickered my "brights" in an attempt to signal the driver that that was a no-no. As I pulled up to a red light, the other car was there. The driver, a young man, rolled down his window and asked, "Did you flicker your brights at me?" I said, "Yes, I did." He asked, "Do you have a problem?" I said, "Yes, I do. I have a wife and son that drive through this neighborhood, and the last thing I am looking for is someone like you to barrel through a stop sign and cause them harm." He asked, "So do you want to make something of it?" With that the light changed, I drove away. I hope that, if nothing else, I made a point, but I wasn't going to get into a fight over it. My son once conveyed to me (when he was in driver's ed) that the rule of thumb is to come to a stop and say to yourself, "S-T-O-P!."

On the matter of excessive speeding, a while ago, I saw a car split in half along the highway. Shortly thereafter, I heard that four young people were killed in that accident. It turned out that a seventeen-year-old with a learner's permit was driving the car, and ironically, he was the only survivor. The law reads that a permit driver must have someone in the car over twenty-one years of age. The oldest of the deceased was eighteen. A permit holder can only drive in the state of New York during the hours of 5:00 a.m.–9:00 p.m. The accident occurred around 3:30 a.m. Who is responsible for this tragedy? Can we hold a seventeen-year-old accountable? Could it have been prevented? Was the driver driving with integrity? What about the passengers? Were they acting in a manner that precipitated this accident? Might they too be the cause of this tragedy?

To drink and drive or Not to drink and drive

Here's a funny story: December is the time of the year when the road-blocks come up with great regularity. I would like to share a personal experience with some of my friends about drinking and driving. (As you well know, some of us have been known to have had brushes with the authorities on our way home from an occasional social session over the years.) A couple of nights ago, I was out for an evening and had quite a few cocktails. Knowing full well I may have been slightly over the limit, I did something I've never done before. I took a cab home. Sure enough, I passed a police roadblock, but since it was a cab, they waved it past. I arrived home safely without incident, which was a real surprise as I have never driven a cab before and am not sure where I got it or what to do with it now that it's in my garage.

Now let's not take this lightly. It may be humorous; however, have you have ever experienced waking up in the morning not remembering how you got home? Not remembering what you did the night before? Think about the consequences. Does your livelihood depend on your driving around? What if you did get stopped? What if you took someone's life along the way? What kind of property damage might you have caused?

Today, in many counties, your car might be impounded and the cost of getting it back is financially very steep.

If you arrived home safely and lives were spared, you got lucky one more time.

* * *

The cost of legal defense, counseling, and fines associated with DWI are enormous. The reward is not worth the risk. There are other alternatives for driving while under the influence, such as taking a cab, calling a friend or perhaps a family member. Think ahead if you're going to be drinking. Is there a hotel or motel nearby?

Do You Speed Excessively?

The speed limit was forty miles per hour on a side road heading to the shopping mall. I looked in my rearview mirror as I normally do. There was a black Nissan zigzagging between cars at about sixty-five–seventy miles per hour. A car was in front of me on the right. As the Nissan approached, I slowed down just in time for him to cut between me and the car in front. He missed me and just missed the other car by a hair. It was a good thing that I slowed down in anticipation of his maneuver or all three cars would have been road kill. The Nissan cut to the right in front of the car ahead of me. About one hundred yards ahead, the light changed to red, and the Nissan came to an abrupt halt. I often wonder what the need is to race down a local road. Where did it get the other driver? What chances did he take that could have cost several people great anguish?

Not Stopping at Stop Signs?

Do you stop at a stop sign, roll through it, or blatantly ignore it sometimes because you think nobody is coming or nobody is watching?

It's downright dangerous when another driver passes through a stop sign. It's not just about being courteous to the next guy. As a New York City driver, I learned that sometimes you have to be an aggressive driver to survive. I was told, "Drive like a cabby."

While on vacation several years ago, driving through the wine country in Napa, California, I was flabbergasted when I came to a three-way intersection. There at the intersection, I couldn't believe my eyes.

I must have been the tenth car in line. At each of the three stops were about the same. Each car came to a complete stop as each driver alternated in sequence. Amazing to my eyes!

After my vacation, once I came back to New York, I applied that theology and changed my approach to lessen my aggressive driving.

My mom and dad live in Boca Raton, Florida, where you see cars coming down the road but don't see the drivers. The older people are either sitting on telephone books or were too short to see over the dashboard. I guess you can say that driving anywhere south of Delray Beach and Boca, or in any area down there, is taking their life into their own hands when they drive. Actually, I think that one day soon, Florida is going to sink because all the old people keep moving there for the warm weather. Traffic is only getting worse.

As my parents age, it has been a concern of mine to monitor their driving habits. When I visit, I take my life in my hands by allowing them to drive so that I can assess their driving ability. I know that the day will come when I feel that they are no longer capable of driving safely. I try to instill the notion of driving with integrity as I monitor them.

One day as we were driving through the development to the club-house about one and a half miles from their home, my dad went through the stop sign around the corner from their home. I yelled, "Dad, you just went through a stop sign." His response was, "It's pretty stupid. There is no need for that sign here." Now, I ask him to say S-T-O-P when he comes to a sign.

If you have elderly parents that you do not want to confront about their unsafe driving, here's a simple hint: I learned that if you anonymously report someone (you can just report their license plate) for unsafe driving on several occasions, the DMV will send a notice to their home, requiring them to take a road test. If they fail, their license will be revoked, and they cannot take another test for six months.

One-Way Street

I will never forget when my dad came up a one-way street the wrong way. We were going to a restaurant. In my car were my wife, my son, and my mom while my dad and daughter went in his car. Neither car was large enough for us all. I got to the restaurant first and parked my car. After we got out, I was watching for my dad. There was a three-lane street in front of us. All of a sudden, I saw him driving past the restaurant. He pulled into another parking lot and asked the attendant where the restaurant was. The attendant pointed back to where we were. My dad proceeded to turn out of the lot and drive the wrong way back to where we were.

I held my breath and thought that that was the end. When he finally parked and exited the car, I approached him and asked him if he was aware of what he just did.

His response was, "There were no other cars coming. What's the big deal?"

How many times are we hearing about devastating accidents that have been occurring lately about people driving the wrong way on a highway or one-way street? There was a limo driver whose passenger

was a young girl, people turning onto the highway at a wrong junc-
ture, too much drinking and driving and just not paying attention.

It's lethal and it has become too prevalent.

Drive safely!!!

Would You Walk a Mile for a Camel or for a Cup of Coffee?

I often stop at Dunkin' Donuts to grab my scooped out whole wheat bagel with bacon, egg, and cheese. Sometimes, I have to walk about a hundred feet to find a parking spot. It's not like there aren't one hundred parking spots within one hundred yards. Although I feel that we are not here to criticize others, I become appalled at the people who park in handicapped spots without handicapped stickers and on fire zones in front of the store. The odd thing is that most of them leave their cars running (with nobody else inside) while they go into the store, leaving their vehicles in a no-park zone, inviting someone to steal it. The best part is that most of these people could use the exercise of walking from a legal parking spot to their destination(s).

I pulled into a parking spot in front of a Starbucks to meet a business associate for coffee one morning. As I was entering, a lady pulled up in front of the door and parked her car there. There was a parking spot about fifty feet away. As she rushed out of her car behind me, I asked her why she left her car there instead of parking it in a parking spot fifty feet away. She said she was in a hurry. I told her that, just like her, all nine people in front of us were probably in a hurry too. Evidently, she got pissed off at me and said something nasty, so I told her she looked a little chunky and probably could have used the extra walk. I don't think she will ever park like that again, do you?

I think the next time she will walk a mile before she parks at the curb.

Teach your children to drive with integrity. They learn from the things you do. How do you set an example for them?

Great Moments Are Made from Great Opportunities

A good indication that you're on the right path is when you start to see more of your trash. You start noticing the ego at play and how you allow it to take hold of you and in your interactions with others.

Seeing our own trash is never easy, but it's what we do once we take notice of the things that tear you down. It makes all the difference.

Getting down, depressed or sad won't help us to change it, so that's a waste of time. On the other hand, we could feel grateful for having the clarity to see what it is we need to change so our lives can improve.

One must remember that even with our negativity, ego, selfishness sometimes getting in the way, we are still always capable.

Sometimes, the negative side creeps in and whispers, "Look at you. You're selfish. You're reactive. You're only human. You can't do it."

It's in moments like these, we need to speak to that voice and tell it, "I know I'm selfish. I know I can be reactive. But I still believe I can do anything. I still believe I can do more." And you can by reaching down deep into your own soul and finding the personal integrity that you contain within yourself.

If it's not one thing, it's another, right? Sometimes we feel like as soon as we're done battling one challenge, another one lands on our plate. It's enough to make us wonder, "Does life ever get any easier?"

Challenges are our greatest opportunities to reveal positive results. When there's more effort required, it only means there will be more fulfillment when we overcome them. Life's lessons have to do with the greater the challenge, the greater the accomplishment.

> *In the middle of difficulty lies opportunity.*
> *Albert Einstein*

What Is Your Ultimate Goal in Life?

My dear friend and accountant, Joseph Scarpa, always says to me, "The obvious isn't always obvious." He's dead on...

During our coaching sessions, Pete (my coach) introduced me to a movie called Peaceful Warrior, one of my favorite motivational flicks. It is the true story about Dan Millman, a world-class gymnast whose goal in life is to qualify for the Olympics and win the gold medal in gymnastics. This is an inspiring movie with many lessons to be learned. This slow-moving, yet highly inspiring movie is about Dan's quest. He meets Socrates, a service station attendant, played by the most unlikely candidate for a film of this nature, Nick Nolte. Socrates teaches Dan that life is a journey. You have to open your mind and take out the trash. He shows Dan how life's long lesson is just that "it's about the journey, not the destination." It's a lesson we all need to be aware of.

* * *

Is your goal in keeping with your life's plan or are you looking at the destination and passing up the journey?

Are you looking toward where you see yourself in the end or are you savoring every step of the way?

You could be passing life by and spending time but wouldn't you care to be doing something worthwhile in giving your life greater value?

When you create value in your life, you are stepping up your level of integrity to yourself.

There's been a lot written on the theme of failure and how integral it is to succeed. In a world where people's value is all too often determined by lists of accomplishments and tangible success, failing feels dangerous.

Many of the greatest people in history were considered least likely to succeed. These people were inventors, leaders, scholars, athletes, and even dreamers. They each started with an idea, which, if they had given up at any point, their failures, instead of leading to great successes, might have been just that, failures. Perseverance, drive, and the undying drive to succeed allowed these people to have made the greatest achievements of our lifetime. Could you imagine if Thomas Edison gave up after his 367th attempt? It wasn't till he had 999 failures that his 1,000th lead to the light bulb as we know it today.

* * *

Eleven Famous Successes That Stemmed From Failure

by Peter Legge, BCBusiness, November 4, 2010

Here is a Who's Who of famous failures that have led to great success stories.

The pursuit of success is full of some failures. In fact, the more we fail, the greater our success. History is chock-a-block full of people who might never have made a success of their lives without some big challenges.

* * *

Zig Ziglar once said, **"Failure is an event, not a person."**

See if you can figure out who's who in these descriptions. (Answers found at bottom of the page.)

a)   He failed the sixth grade and was defeated in every single election for public office until he became Prime Minister at the young age of 62.

b)   He was booed from the podium when he first released his ideas and was considered an outcast by his peers and the scientific community.

c)   In the first year of her contract, she was dropped by her producers because they thought she was unattractive and couldn't act.

d)   He did not speak until he was four years old, and couldn't read until he was seven. His parents thought he was "sub-normal." He was expelled from school and his teachers described him as "mentally slow, unsociable and a drip forever in foolish dreams."

e) He was fired after his first performance at the Grand Ole Opry and told by the manager, "You ain't going nowhere son, you otta go back to driving a truck."

f) She was broke, living on welfare, severely depressed, divorced and a single mother while attending school and attempting to write her first novel.

g) After a screen test, the memo from the director read, "can't act, can't sing, slightly bald, can dance...a little."

h) A professor suggested he drop out of the English department and college altogether. At his very first job, he was paid in cases of shaving cream, soda, and nail clippers. His first book was rejected by 27 publishers before printers accepted it

i) Enduring a rough and often abusive childhood, she faced numerous career setbacks including being fired from her first job because she was unfit for TV.

j) He was told by Emperor Ferdinand that his operas were "far too noisy" and contained "far too many notes."

k) They said he was too small and didn't skate well enough. Yet, he set the standard for grit, courage, skill and humility.

Answers: A) Winston Churchill; B) Sigmund Freud; C) Marilyn Monroe; D) Albert Einstein; E) Elvis Presley; F) J.K. Rowling; G) Fred Astaire; H) Dr. Seuss; I) Oprah Winfrey; J) Wolfgang Mozart; K) Stan "Steamer" Smyl - Vancouver Canucks.

Note: If you never fail, you'll never succeed.

Vicky, the Turkey Lady: Quite an inspiration

Woman who was kept in coma for a month after being hit by flying frozen turkey forgives teenager for prank by Sara Nelson, Daily Mail Online, 10 November 2010, 09:37 EST

Many of you may have heard the story about a group of teenagers who bought a frozen turkey, using a stolen credit card, in 2004. The group was driving around when one of them decided to throw it out the moving vehicle's window. Nearly every bone in Victoria Ruvolo's face was broken after the missile smashed through her car windshield and nearly killed her. The 50-year-old woman whose face had to be completely rebuilt after she was hit in the face by a frozen 20lb turkey has forgiven her assailant.

Victoria suffered a horrendous aftermath as doctors were forced to keep her in a medically induced coma for almost a month after the incident, in Long Island, Lake Ronkonkoma.

"I was one block from my house. I didn't wake up for almost a month."

Ruvolo, whose survival was described by doctors as a 'miracle', endured many surgeries and now has three titanium plates in her face. But despite her brush with death Ruvolo pleaded for mercy on behalf of the assailant, who received just six months in jail, followed by five-year' probation.

She said: "If I hadn't let go of that anger I'd be consumed by this need for revenge. "Forgiving him helps me move on. "I told him: 'Just do something with your life,' and then I hugged him."

Ruvolo, who now volunteers with a probation department, has kept her sense of humor despite her ordeal. She admitted: "I'm trying to help others, but I know for the rest of my life I'll be known as The Turkey Lady. "Could have been worse. He could have thrown a ham. I'd be Miss Piggy!!!

Integrity versus Obsession

When you spend more time working your life away rather than enjoying your life, your family, friends, and the adventure that each day brings what is the value of your being?

We tend to live in the past or in the future.

There are people who live in the past, focus on previous achievements, holding onto childhood trauma so much that they feel they are still there today.

Others live in the future, existing in a sort of dreamland, telling everyone what great person they're going to be or what incredible feats they are going to accomplish. Both of these states, past, and future, are simply ways of escaping responsibilities in the present.

Being Present

Being there for people means being fully in the present for them physically, mentally, spiritually, and emotionally as well. Sometimes we pretend to be there, but in our minds, we might be thinking of all the things we have to do.

Self-Talk

The more we talk, the more we become unaware of what's being said and all that is happening around us. We disconnect from the bigger picture.

By the way, this goes not just for talking out loud but talking in our heads too! Many of us may be quiet externally but spend all day talking to ourselves in our heads.

We all want to do what we want to do when we want to do it, but when we have a chance to step out of our own agenda and do what someone else wants, that is our golden opportunity to bring the light into our lives.

Negative Self Talk

Did you ever talk yourself out of something you wanted to do or accomplish? Yes, you did. When a golfer takes a shot and there is water in front of him/her there is a natural tendency to think "I don't want to hit the ball in the water," When a baseball player gets up at bat and thinks to himself "I don't want to strike out," When there is a big business deal on the table and you start to think "I hope the bank doesn't fail me," you're planting all the wrong seeds.

My dear friend Dan Schaefer, PhD. has a company called Peak Performance. He assists people in being more successful by getting rid of the negative self-talk. Dr. Dan works with professional athletes, business people, people taking specialized exams to created positive results. In his book CLICK! The Competitive Edge he discusses many ways to improve your position. www.PeakPerformanceStrategies.com

Sharing Responsibilities

Well, like a good partner and sharing husband, either my wife or I cook the meals, and I do the dishes while she puts the food away (unless I can coerce my son to do the dishes). I was brought up in a home (and by my wife too) where we washed the dishes before we put them into the dishwasher to remove the food particles. So in case you don't run the dishwasher that day, you don't keep crusty and cruddy dishes hanging around. It's the same principal, I guess, like when my mom would clean the house before the cleaning girls showed up. Just in case they didn't do a good job. Dishes are one thing, but then there are the pots and pans. It always seems that when it's my turn to wash the dishes, there are more pots and pans. I notice the crud that was left on the pots from the previous time they were washed (I didn't do them). It's one thing to say they're washed versus getting them to spotlessly shine. What's the difference?

When you spend the appropriate time necessary to do a job (any job) as best as it can be done, which, in this case (and also in many other situations), does not require much more effort than when you do it so haphazardly. It doesn't take that much more effort to do the job well.

Doing the dishes is like anything in life. You can do a superior job or you can find gravy stains and pieces of veggies on the pan when you cook your next meal. You can make sure all your ducks are in a row and nothing is going to bite you in the ass, or you can have sleepless nights thinking about the mess you still have to clean up.

* * *

Does Your Accountant Have Integrity?

Does your accountant show you ways to cheat on your taxes or is it the loopholes that are allowed? The American Institute of Certified Public Accountants (AICPA) is a professional organization responsible for developing professional ethical values in accounting. The AICPA requires professional accountants to act responsibly when engaging in accounting services and reviewing sensitive financial information. Accountants should always exercise sound moral judgment in all accounting activities. Accountants have the unique responsibility of providing clients with professional services while presenting a truthful and accurate assessment of a company's financial health to the general public. However, is that always the case?

There are many accountants that look the other way for their clients to save them on paying taxes. They ask their clients to send them a written inventory or a written statement for the accountant to submit so that although the accountant is doing an ethical job using the numbers, it is the numbers their clients are supplying rather than actual book numbers. If a problem arises, the accountant can say, "But those are the numbers my client gave me." He has done an accurate job using what the client supplied. Is this ethical or not ethical?

My CPA is one of the most ethical people I know and certainly trust. If anything, he goes the other way to protect my interests.

Integrity is an important fundamental element in the accounting profession. It requires accountants, to be honest, candid, and forthright with a client's financial information. Accountants should restrict themselves from personal gain or advantage by using confidential information.

While errors or differences in opinion regarding the applicability of accounting laws do exist, professional accountants should avoid the intentional opportunity to deceive and manipulate financial information.

Due care is the ethical value requiring accountants to observe all technical or ethical accounting standards. Professional accountants are often required to review generally accepted accounting principles (GAAP) and apply this framework to a company's specific financial information. Due care requires accountants to exercise competence, diligence, and a proper understanding of financial information. Competence is usually based on an individual's education and experience. Thus, due care may require senior accountants to supervise and direct other accountants with less experience in the accounting profession.

* * *

Is Your Financial Advisor an Asset or a Liability?

Your friend is depending on your investment to get his business up and running. You agreed to help your friend move. You made a large pledge, but circumstances have since changed. Just how binding are your commitments? When is it all right to renege?

Is it a tool to help you retain and gain more funds so that you maintain the healthiest and wealthiest portfolio that will take you through your retirement?

Does your financial advisor treat you like a client or a profit center?

My aunt is ninety years old and single. My uncle passed away five years ago, leaving my aunt with no idea of their financial state of affairs. My uncle was a very frugal person. As an engineer, he was always meticulous and precise. He seemed to always have a cold and mysterious aura about him, yet he was always a very loving person. My aunt worked as a travel agent and assorted other jobs to earn whatever little she could to supplement the family income. She was what (in the Jewish faith) might call a bala Busta. Selma knew everything about everybody and was a true connector who always was trying to make marriages between others. She was always interested in other people and only in a very genuine way yet getting a hug from her was rare. Throughout their fifty-nine years of marriage, my aunt always believed that she and my uncle were always struggling to make ends meet. My cousins always envied my family because my dad always had nice cars, a nice house, and seemed to have money. My aunt and uncle always drove an older car, they lived in a garden apartment and never went on extravagant vacations, nor did they eat in fancy restaurants. Selma never shopped in regular clothing stores. She frequented thrift shops, bazaars, and discount stores; and she was a hoarder. It's a funny story, but my aunt could never turn down a bargain. Whenever she went into a bazaar or thrift store and found a ridiculous sale, she bought those items. If she was going to someone's home or it was someone's birthday (even strangers), she always had a gift to give. Whenever we went into their garage, you had to walk in between the aisles. There were medicine cabinets, dolls, clothing, clocks, and anything you could imagine piled up to the ceiling in Selma's garage.

So here we are in 2009 when Lester passed away. My aunt is freaking out because she believes she is destitute and has no money. Several month's had passed, and Selma had never let her two daughters nor my father (her brother) help her sort out her finances until one day when Selma got seriously ill. At that time, she and her daughters began to sort out the papers. Selma asked my father for some advice. My father, who is financially savvy, began to go over Lester's notes and papers to find that Selma was worth in excess of two million plus dollars. Selma then decided to go out and find her own financial advisor. She went to a seminar where there was a free dinner. At that event, she met a nice-looking young man who seemed to have great knowledge of the financial world. This good-looking financial advisor won over Selma's heart and her account too. She signed a power of attorney to him to do what he felt best with her account. She trusted him. Within a few short months, he had Selma's portfolio together and invested as he saw fit. As time passed and after several discussions, Selma told Murray, my dad, about some of the dividends she was receiving and that she was a little concerned about the amounts she was receiving. When Murray went over the portfolio, he found Selma was supposed to be receiving larger dividend checks from some of the investments that were made to the tune of about $60,000 a year. It seemed that many of the investments that the financial advisor had placed Selma's money in were paying him higher commissions. He kept on moving monies around into other funds so that he could receive greater commissions. He was churning her accounts.

What was his level of integrity? It was not looking out for the better interest of his client; it was to better his own personal interest. Is your financial advisor up to date with all of the latest insurance products on the market and is he/she well versed in these products so that they can advise you which product is more beneficial to suit your financial needs.

By the way, Selma, now past age 90, is one of the sharpest bulbs in the tree today when it comes to her finances and investments.

There are multiple companies offering such a large variety of insurance, i.e., long-term care policies, long-term care policies that are convertible life, etc. Without the proper advice, even the most prudent person would not know which policy to choose.

Does your advisor discuss the employee retirement plans available to you and charge excessive fees that are eroding your retirement savings?

Make sure that the person that you are putting your trust in is the person that you can put your financial future with.

Purity in Innocence

It seems as though whenever I travel to a new city, someplace new, I feel a certain paranoia that makes me a bit uneasy. When I travel out in the country or in the mountains, it offers a serenity that calms my soul, but I guess it has to do much with the feeling that you have to adapt to change. You have to grasp the nuances in your mind.

One morning, I was walking in Manhattan, a Japanese girl, obviously, a first-time tourist in New York City, came running out of the Marriott Residence Inn on Sixth Avenue near Thirty-Ninth Street, holding a camera and giggling with excitement as she began taking pictures of all the buildings snap after snap. It appeared to me that she must have arrived the evening before. Her excitement and innocence grabbed me. Here was someone so intrigued and immersed in her excitement that there was a sense of innocence and purity in her actions.

The purity of thought and mind is something that, if we can achieve and adds integrity to our souls. It helps us expand our senses in the purest form so that we can find our true inner self. In my readings and exploration of the Kabbalah and Eastern philosophy, particularly the Autobiography of a Yogi, the teachings of the Paramahansa Yogananda I learned that this is so.

So You Wanted a Pet...Really?

You've decided you needed a pal to hang with because you were lonely. You need someone or something to sleep with and to keep you company, someone to play with, in your time of need. Different pets satisfy different needs in people. Whether you're selecting to have a dog or cat, goldfish or a turtle, a ferret or a bunny rabbit, different pets have different levels of care; and there is always some sort of cost whether it is time or money. You must be prepared to understand the costs whether you are a child or an adult. Sometimes people do not think hard enough about the association of cost to benefit.

Selecting the right breed or species is essential in order to adapt to your surroundings. Do investigation and research! You don't want a Bernese mountain dog in an efficiency apartment in Manhattan or a bull in a china shop. You can't mix fresh-water fish with salt-water fish, and you can't put a bird in a cage with a cat.

Pets are like humans too; they have needs and feelings, and they depend on their owners to be devoted to their care. They need time to play, and just as plants need water, the sunshine, and food, pets need to be walked, fed, and played with.

Your pets require going to the vet for checkups, and like children, there are many times when they get sick or need further attention.

The cost of food, toys, blankets, resolve to clean up the pee and poo stains, vitamins, and medications can be expensive. Nothing comes cheap.

You need to make plans when you go on vacation, whether to take your pet or make arrangements with someone for their care. Too many people get pets from breeders or shelters with good intention but without thinking about the reality of commitment.

Having a pet requires an integrity commitment.

Do You Enjoy Waiting for the Doctor?

Making an appointment weeks in advance, so you can spend an hour in the waiting room and fifteen minutes with the doctor, is such a totally awesome adventure. At least, I get time to read, that I don't usually have. Personally, I book the first appointment at 8:00 a.m., so don't get held back because of delays in other appointments or emergencies the doctor might have during the day. I get there fifteen minutes early in anticipation that I might be called in early. Ha! So I sit there in the waiting room. After inquiring with the receptionist twice, I get called into the examination (holding) room and wait fifteen minutes for the nurse practitioner who takes my vitals. I then sit there for fifteen–twenty minutes until the doctor comes in. He reads the chart and says, "Hum! How are you feeling?" They spend 5 minutes with you and hands you back to the nurse-practioner. Pissed Off !!! My blood pressure went through the roof.

* * *

Integrity of Our Food Supply...and Coding-Diet

by Tami Racaniello, personal training, and wellness coach

Tami Racaniello of It's Time to Get Fit Inc., through a commitment to herself and having the integrity to do what is right, burned a path to health through testing the integrity of our food supply and coding by challenging the labeling on products.

How important is it that we keep a proper diet? The foods we eat make a difference in how we feel and how we act and react. Everything we put into our bodies interacts with our metabolism and our blood and creates chemical changes.

Every obstacle we stumble upon, every challenge we experience in our lives is actually nothing more than opportunity—the greatest opportunity in fact—to reveal light in our lives. We are meant to use our challenges and know that if we can overcome them, we can overcome anything.

Greatness is not about what we achieve. It's about what we overcome.

Tami Racaniello spent most of her life unhealthy, overweight, and in the care of a doctor for one ailment or another. At the age of forty, Tami embarked on a soul-searching journey and in a quest for a healthier lifestyle. By developing a positive mindset, better self-esteem, changing to a more plant-based diet, and discovering the joys of exercise and weight lifting, Tami lost over one hundred pounds. Her experience was so profound that it became her mission to inspire others to make positive changes to their life and health.

Now at the age of fifty, Tami holds certifications in personal training, yoga, Pilates, Reiki, wellness coaching, nutrition, cooking (raw food/vegan), and CPR, and keeps the educational process going by taking classes and getting certifications on a regular basis to be the best possible source of information for her clients.

Tami's clients love that she makes it easy to be healthy with small manageable steps that they can take every day to improve their health and body composition and reverse the aging process.

Making it easy to be healthy is what Tami is really great at! For people that don't have time to get to the gym, she develops exercises that can be done anywhere at any time, even in the workplace. She will specially tailor healthy menus for client's favorite restaurant, so ordering a nutrition-packed meal becomes a no-brainer, and she teaches the concept of intuitive eating for optimal nutrition and to combat food cravings.

For clients that have tried numerous programs with no lasting results, that need a more focused approach, or feel that better health is unattainable, Tami is a hands-on cheerleader and motivator, empowering those clients to overcome obstacles to achieve their goals.

Tami gives corporate presentations on how to be healthy in the workplace and beyond, and also offers Smoothie Afternoons, a unique alternative to the afternoon sugar crave. She provides holistic services to people undergoing cancer treatments, works with a number of nonprofit organizations offering health programs, and leads crowd warm-ups at fundraising walks. Tami is a published author in magazines, online, and in books. She writes:

How important is it that we keep a proper diet? The foods we eat make a difference in how we feel and how we act and react.

When you eat, you extract, process, and absorb the life-sustaining energy from the food, otherwise known as the digestive process. It's really mind-blowing to think of digesting food in this way, but it honors the connection between what we eat and how we feel. The saying, "You are what you eat", is true. The quality of the food you consume determines the health and quality of your life.

How often do you eat foods that don't honor what your body needs in the name of celebration? When you really want something that's not nutritious for your body, truly enjoy that food and move on. Call those items treats, not cheats. Cheating means something sneaky or dishonest. The way you think about the food you consume also matters in how you feel after you eat it.

What you eat can be a result of your mood, or your mood can be a result of the food you eat. If you're stressed or upset, you may want comfort food, chocolate or something crunchy and salty. If you have a processed carbohydrate for breakfast, such as a bagel or muffin, in a couple of hours you may feel cranky or tired due to the drop in your blood sugar. Both situations have a chemical effect on the balance of the body. Our body naturally has internal mechanisms for creating balance to maintain health. Help those mechanisms function optimally by providing quality nutrition.

There is so much health and nutrition information out there. The diet industry, the internet, magazines, books, our neighbors and friends all have the "answer" to what we should eat or take to be healthy. As a Coach, there needs to be a certain level of integrity, especially where someone's health is concerned. There is so much more to consider besides weight loss. Does the person have health issues? What reaction will it have on the individual? What kind of support is given?

Many diet programs tend to separate weight loss and health when they should be considered together. Making conscious choices for your needs boosts your mental and physical health. Addressing stress levels, making time for things you enjoy, finding a spiritual connection, and having a good support system are key to long-lasting health. Weight loss is a positive byproduct of having all those things in place.

Your attitude and belief about yourself, determine the choices you make in what you eat. Stable and lasting changes in your way of eating, occur step by step, not all at once. When you begin to observe your food choices without judgment, you begin to pay attention to your own inner messages and how you feel after eating various foods. You sense which foods support you and make you feel better, and no longer eat unconsciously to meet your emotional needs. Instead, you start to make conscious choices that make you feel better and honor your spirit.

Remember, this is your journey. Take it at your own pace, following your own inner guidance. Honor, love, and respect yourself, without being critical or quick to judge. Learn from your experiences and understand why you made your choices so you can transform your life and health by bringing more harmony, peace, and balance into your life. As you experience a more positive way of being, you will have a better understanding of what nourishes, satisfies, and supports you. You learn to honor yourself and support your growth by choosing the foods, thoughts, and behaviors that nourish and heal your body. Your mind, body and spirit will work in harmony to support you and enable you to consciously make healthy choices because you are what you eat. www.itstimetoget fit.com

Are Reporters Telling
Us the Real News?

Today, it's all about readership, sensationalism, how many viewers you can capture with a headline. Every radio station, newspaper and television station reports the news as they want you to hear it. The political views, gory details of a 10 car collision, driveby shootings or tornado destruction are used to sell air-time and headlines. Sensationalism sells advertising space.

Reporters are gathering interviews and calling in the news as they see it or as they hear it. We have all been told that there are 3 sides to every story. In a day where improper reporting can be a liability, reporters are no longer recording all the information, they are interpreting it, as they see it.

Stephen Carter says, "I have gone half mad in interviews, watching the journalists' pen scratch, stop scratching, scratch, stop scratching, often stopping, perhaps to rest aching fingers, just when I am trying to explain a crucial point. I once said to her reporter, 'Please write down this part,' and she looked at me with that special First Amendment arrogance that every journalist can do at the drop of a hat, not denying to reply with what she was obviously thinking, 'Don't you dare tell me how to do my job."

What's happening with today's television shows? Have talk shows gone too far? Are reality shows real? To pin the responsibility of how today's society reacts to the shows of this nature only shows the lack of integrity that we have today. The shows, although highly profitable by selling to their audiences in the desire to shock, deliberately create provocative situations, knowing—indeed, I suspect, hoping—that some guests, and some viewers, will fly into paroxysms of anger, sorrow, pain, guilt, joy, whatever that makes such fabulous television. And the media industry understands it perfectly well that you motion all pornography is where the money is.

Dedications to My Heroes

My father, Murray Soskil, is a real hero. It has been sixty years since WWII. At the age of eighty-two, he began to write his memoirs and his activities in World War II. Through the process of editing and working with my dad on his project, I developed a new sense of respect for the US military and those who are willing to die and offer their service, defending our country. Through another project that I was involved in (which I shared in this book), I was able to make contact with the Wounded Warrior Project, which bestowed me the privilege to have my father honored on May 5, 2012, at Citi Field during a New York Mets game. My dad's book, From the Bronx to Berchtesgaden: Memoir of a World War II Hero, was published and has sold thousands of copies on Amazon. His works have become a great inspiration to many.

After the completion and even during my editing of his book, I didn't realize the role my dad made during the war. Through the Veteran of the Game process, I found out more about a piece of his life that he had kept to himself for almost seventy years. As a recipient of two Silver Stars, Bronze Star, eight Battle Stars, Presidential Unit Citation, French Foligiere, French medal of valor, sharpshooter award, and several other medals that had been stolen from him. My father was always humble and never explained to us what these awards represented or why he received them; however, he kept them hidden and wore his pride within. Since that time, I have been spreading the word about the Wounded Warrior Project to create more awareness for our wounded heroes, our veterans, and our armed forces. Dad passed on September 11, 2013, the day of the unsung hero.

I thank my mother, Pearl, whose strength and countenance has given me the inner strength to have confidence in myself so that I may always strive to move forward.

My accountant and close friend, Joseph Scarpa, CPA, who is one of the most ethical people you can ever come in contact with, has been my confidant and chief collaborator and has assisted me in more ways than I can think.

Jeffrey Schwartz was my former partner and general counsel for Sluggers Jewels. He believed in me as a friend and business partner and has spent countless hours diligently working and supporting me with his friendship and legal services, his tremendous negotiating skills, business acumen, and encouragement as well as his insight to reach for the stars even if you only catch the moon theology, which has kept me focused and driven me out of my comfort zone at times to do things I could never have done on my own. He had been one of my greatest advocates at that time. His motto consists of three words, Conceive, Believe, and Achieve. Our journey together was a special part of my life.

Thank you, Lawrence "Dutch" Bliss, my wife's cousin Lynn's husband, who I enjoy spending time with. Dutch was always a happy-go-lucky, fun-loving, vibrant man who would give the shirt off his back to help someone in need. Four years ago Dutch suffered a massive stroke. He is an inspiration to all as we watch him fight to be the best he can be. Several years prior, Dutch's grandson, Michael (my next hero), was out with friends at 3:00 a.m., going into a pizza shop where three young men came out and started calling Michael names. One of the guys picked up a pipe and started beating Michael as the others kicked and punched him then they left him beaten on the street. Michael's friends had ran for help, however, too late. Michael was left paralyzed and beaten pretty badly. Over three years had passed during which Dutch took Michael to every possible clinic and spent every waking hour dedicating himself to Michael's slow recovery. He has relentlessly attempted to find ways for Michael to rehabilitate himself. Although Michael has come a long way, he is limited to a wheelchair and will be for the rest of his life. It was attributed to Dutch's efforts that Michael has come so far and to Lynn, my wife's cousin. Lynn's unselfish love has driven her to take care of Dutch by herself while working and running a household. Her endless love and total dedication has drained her and taken her away from having any personal time of her own. She is an inspiration and the meaning of the word love.

My aunt Selma, who always has a smile on her face turning January 9, 2015, is one of the happiest go-lucky people I know. After my uncle passed away, she has dealt with breast cancer, blood disease, broken hip, and yet she visited other elderly people in a nursing home with a friend, dressed as clowns, to make people smile.

I thank Bill (William J.) Corbett P.R. for spending many hours collaborating with me on many of the ideas contained in this book, and my friend, Robert Kothe, president of Faxtback, for assisting me in spreading the word by videotaping me and compiling videos for future references.

Special thank you to Pete Cracovaner, president of the Pinnacle Resource Group, my life coach, my business coach, my friend, and my catalyst for the evolving of this project in its inception (which he was unaware of till now). Whether my quest will make a great impact, or not, on the world, it was Pete who has enlightened me to see that my destination is not dependent on just financial gain but on the journey traveled until I reach my destination. As we all put too much emphasis on the destination, we lose the purpose of the journey.

Pete opened my eyes to learn that the journey is about the experiences that one must live in order to find one's true purpose in life. It is about living through the challenges in life that create new opportunities and open new doors. This quest, like the story of the Knight in Rusty Armor, by Robert Fischer, has given me great knowledge and enabled me to grow in new ways. It has given me a greater sense of spirituality as it might enable me to make a difference in this world. I have already seen the impact that short discussions, which I have had with people, has begun to make some people stop and think about the responsibility of their own actions and the impact they might make on other people too. Although the commencement of our sessions (Pete and I) revealed nothing in regard to this particular project, it led to the substance behind it. Pete reinforced the importance of having gratitude and focusing on my journey. It was his influence, which has gotten me to focus on my tasks. Through a willingness and a sense of pride and a feeling of accomplishment, I am encouraged to complete projects that I otherwise would have left incomplete.

Pete has instilled within me that I have the ability to step out of my comfort zone to deal with situations, people, and challenges that I (like most people) try to avoid because of the fear of success. I have been blessed and I thank our Universal Power, which has given me hope and strength and the ability to be thankful and grateful for what I have through the many adversities that have been put before me.

Although there were many times in my life that I thought no longer offered me hope or promise to go on, the power of the universe has given me a road map so that I may learn from and realized my journey. I learned that age is just a number. It has no capability to prevent you from achieving your dreams at any point in time. As long as you mind is focused on a goal, you can accomplish anything.

Jeffrey Stern, Preident of Eagle Business Solutions took me through the back end of the completion of this book and the development of the business aspect of The Nail Of Integrity, LLC. As a business consultant, Jeff kept my feet on the ground and my mind on the project. Thanks, Jeff.

Shared Stories

Letters

Marvin, I was walking to my car at the end of the day today. Running late with a few boxes in my arms and my briefcase in hand, I was struggling. About 40 feet from my car, I walked over a razor blade. It was just next to the curb, and I just ignored it. I took maybe 5 steps and thought I should pick it up. I walked to my car, remembering that years ago I was driving and heard my tire pop and deflate maybe on 30 seconds. I jumped out of my car to find it sliced open by a razor blade. After putting the boxes in my car, I went back and picked up the razor blade. I probably would not have done this if it were not for speaking with you and discussing integrity. I think that nail of integrity moments are something that people will share with you. Save this and the others that come in. Thank you for reminding me about integrity and remembering to do the right thing. Feel free to share this. Bill Corbett Jr., Corbett Public Relations www.corbetpr.com

From Ronan Yari via Twitter

I have a problem with integrity and I need some help. You know the type. They are always on time, every time and sometimes ahead of time. And if they are going to be late, they let you know. And if they say they are going to do something, it gets done. I always assumed that people that show up on time and keep their word have integrity. But is that always the case? I'm in the business of organizing stuff, adventures, travel, work and all sorts of projects. I come up with ideas and then I literally manage to make them happen. And for them to happen, I need partners with integrity. But integrity is hard to define. For example My partner-in-adventures is my friend Ofer. If you walk into a crowded room, you'd have a hard time finding him. Most likely he'd be in a corner fiddling with some technology, or watching the action from a safe vantage point. But if I needed someone to meet me at the mouth of the Amazon river with a kayak on Thursday at 3:45 PM a year from now, Ofer would be there at 3:15 PM heating up the tea and getting the roof rack unstrapped. That's integrity, but is showing up enough? My partner-in-life is my wife Elizabeth. She shows up on time, but that's not the highlight. Elizabeth is not just about doing the right thing; she's about doing what must be done. This is a subtle but a huge distinction. If a friend is sick, I'll check off my must-do-list: call, send a card or visit. Elizabeth on the other hand, will change the bed sheets, or run out to buy food, or give our friend a shave. Elizabeth would stay until whatever needed to get done got done. That's integrity, but when do you stop? My partner-in-dharma is Roni. She's rarely on time, but those who know Roni, know that Einstein himself would have to rework a few formulas of relativity to calculate the energy per good she puts out to service her community. If you are hurting, if you need a meal, a job, or a roof over your head, she will take you under her wing no matter the time. That's integrity, but it's rarely on time or without risks? My partner-in-commitment is Charlie. Once he takes on a project, nothing will stop him. He single-handedly revived his town's newspaper by putting in 70 hour weeks for several years in order to educate the Andover community and give its citizens a voice. Very few would have taken on this project and none would have survived the long and grueling commitment. But what a gift Charlie bestowed on his community, just because he could. That's integrity, but at what cost? Integrity seems to have a variety of shades. Perhaps integrity is a concept that we strive for but never reach, or maybe we reach it in one aspect of our lives, but not in others. Just showing up on time, or doing the right thing, or giving till no end have elements of integrity, but may not be integrated with the rest of our lives. Tricky stuff, but I think the basic unit of integrity is nothing more and nothing less than a person's word. For a person to have integrity, his word must be whole, complete, unbroken, sound and in perfect condition.

Online Comments:

Peter Pitzele · Hotchkiss High School If integrity is one end of the spectrum what's at the other? And is there a word that is the opposite of integrity that is not pejorative? And is there a kind of integrity that isn't always a positive?

Ronen Yaari I guess if the word integration is part of integrity, then the opposite of integration is apart, where not all the pieces are working together. That is what's puzzling - in some aspects of my life I have integrity and in some I don't. That is why I'm thinking this is a work in progress. Can you give examples of integrity that is negative?

Lisa C Mendelsund · Works at Bhava Yoga Brattleboro I think of Integrity as "Integer" or whole, like in our 24th week when our arm buds descend the heart and lungs and the leg-flippers fan out from the guts....before the tendrils of our Projects and relations and views made us a mass of disassociated parts. Integrity is for me, when my actions are hooked into something centralized and not operating in the distil channels of surface provocations etc. love.

Susan Lichtenstein · Top Commenter · Broker/Sales Representative at Gold star/real living To me it means "TRUST"…Obviously there is more to it but that is the one word that I have if you can only use one.

Liat Jarkon Horlick Humility, patience, and understanding toward others who may not meet your expectations or standards… An opinion: set goals not expectations the search for "perfection" is futile… the search for self-improvement

Suzin Varro · Certified Lead Photographer at Lifetouch National School Studios I feel integrity can be defined by this slogan, "Say what you mean, and mean what you say." Greg and I are super-social people—we will meet complete strangers and engage in deep conversations and connect and exchange contacts—the people we meet are so enthusiastic about staying in touch—but we never hear from them again. Saying one thing—doing another. Lack of integrity?

Ronen Yaari I guess there is a subtle difference between being polite and giving your word. I think the people that come through with what they say over and over, even casually, really stand out. Maybe the lesson here is, if you don't mean it…hold your tongue.

Conclusion

It's amazing what happens when you recognize your good qualities, accept responsibility for your future, and take positive action to make that future even brighter.
Zig Zigler

* * *

After the cheers have died and the stadium is empty, after the headlines have been written and after you are back in the quiet of your own room, and the Super Bowl ring has been placed on the dresser, and all the pomp and fanfare has faded, the enduring things that are left is the dedication to doing with our lives the very best we can to make the world a better place in which to live."
Vince Lombardi

* * *

Let's strive to make the world a better place in which to live.

Thank you,

Marvin Soskil, Author

Bibliography

Preface

"To thine own self-be true"
Shakespeare, William. *Hamlet*, Act 1, Scene III.

"You must take personal responsibility for your life."
Rohn, Jim. BrainyQuote.com, Xplore Inc, 2016. http://www.brainy-quote.com/quotes/quotes/j/jimrohn133626.html.

"Taking responsibility for your behavior"
Tuchman, Barbara M. in Kidder, Rushworth M. and others. *An Agenda for the 21st Century*. Cambridge, Massachusetts: The MIT Press, 1987.

"It is not what we eat"
Bacon, Francis, in *Wisdom for the Soul*, edited by Larry Chang. Washington D. C.: Gnosophia Publishers, 2006.

Introduction

"You're either living in the problem"
Proctor, Bob. AZQuotes.com, Wind and Fly LTD, 2016. http://www.azquotes.com/quote/1268296.

Do You Believe in a Higher Power?

"As we look around us these days"
"Interview with Yehuda Berg." *USA Talk Today*, May 27, 2004.

"The age group most at risk"
Smola, Jennifer. "Study: Cell phone-related pedestrian injuries soar."
USA TODAY, September 17, 2013.

Dichotomy of a Nail

"Just as the nail will hold"
Attributed to Robert Kothe.

"We switch on our favorite nightly news program"
Walker, Paul L. *The Ministry of Church and Pastor*. Pathway Press, 1965.

What Is Integrity?

"The most influential tool"
Attributed to Zig Ziglar.
Stone, Dave. Refining Your Style: Learning from Respected
Communicators. Group Pub Inc. 2004.

Definition of Integrity

"integrity"
Dictionary.com. Denis Howe. http://dictionary.reference.com/
browse/integrity.

"Each of us will someday be judged"
Attributed to William Arthur Ward.
Ziglar, Zig. *Over the to*p. Thomas Nelson: Nashville. 1997.

Integrity Is Destiny

"Character gets you out of bed"
Ziglar, Zig. *Over the to*p. Thomas Nelson: Nashville. 1997.

"The soul is dyed the color of its thoughts"
Attributed to Heraclitus.

Be Who You Are and Be True to Your Core Beliefs

"Operating from the center of one's being"
Cloud, Henry. *Integrity, the Courage to Meet the Demands of Reality*.
HarperBusiness: New York. 2009.

"Every move that we make is followed by a consequence"
Gilbert, Daniel. *Stumbling on Happiness*. Vintage. 2007.

"We assume life will go on"
Cialdini, Robert B. *Influence: Science and Practice* (5th Edition). Allyn
and Bacon. 2008.

"The wonderful thing about character and integrity"
"How to Build Character through Integrity." wikiHow. http://www.
wikihow.com/Build-Character-Through-Integrity.

"The ideal man"
Aristotle. *Nicomachean Ethics* (2nd Edition). Hackett Publishing Company, Inc. 1999.

"Happiness cannot be traveled to"
Waitley, Denis. BrainyQuote.com, Xplore Inc, 2016. http://www.brainyquote.com/quotes/quotes/d/deniswaitl146923.html.

"In this life, we have to make many choices"
Faust, James E. "Choices" The Church of Jesus Christ of Latter-Day Saints, https://www.lds.org/general-conference/2004/04/choices.

"A man does what he must"
Kennedy, John F. BrainyQuote.com, Xplore Inc, 2016. http://www.brainyquote.com/quotes/quotes/j/johnfkenn162486.html.

"We have an innate desire"
Gallozi, Chuck. *The 3 Thieves and 4 Pillars of Happiness: 7 Steps to a Life of Boundless Joy.* Mill City Press, Inc. 2011.

"In order to build any entity"
Carter, Stephen L. *Integrity.* Harper Perennial: New York. 1996.

"I always want them to see"
Cantatore, Felice. *Rocky Spirit: The Rocky Balboa Connection to Success.* IUniverse. 2007.

"We read and discussed"
Fisher, Robert. The Knight in Rusty Armor. Wilshire Book Co. 1987.

"The man who promises everything"
Jung, Carl. BrainyQuote.com, Xplore Inc, 2016. http://www.brainy-quote.com/quotes/quotes/c/carljung157294.html.

"When a person makes a promise"
Smede, Lewis B. "Controlling the Unpredictable—The Power of Promising." *Christianity Today*, January 21, 1983

"In executing the duties"
Washington, George. "From George Washington to the Massachusetts Senate and House of Representatives, 9 July 1789." National Archives, http://founders.archives.gov/documents/Washington/05-03-02-0080.

"Enthusiasm is one of the most powerful"
Emerson, Ralph Waldo. *Selected Writings of Ralph Waldo Emerson*. Signet Reprint. 2011.

"The discipline you learn"
Bennett, Bo. BrainyQuote.com, Xplore Inc, 2016. http://www.brainyquote.com/quotes/quotes/b/bobennett167493.html.

"True discipline"
Attributed to Sybil Stanton.
Ziglar, Zig. *Over the top*. Thomas Nelson: Nashville. 1997.

"When children of my generation"
Carter, Stephen L. *Integrity*. Harper Perennial: New York. 1996.

"When you look in the mirror"
Icke, David. BrainyQuote.com, Xplore Inc, 2016. http://www.brainyquote.com/quotes/quotes/d/davidicke543061.html.

"Anything that we are aware of"
The Blackwell Companion to Consciousness, edited by Max Velmans and Susan Schneider. Blackwell Publishing. 2007.

"The subconscious mind stores information"
"Subconscious." Psychology Wiki. http://psychology.wikia.com/wiki/Subconscious.

"I think that there's something in the American "
Michael Moore. AZQuotes.com, Wind and Fly LTD, 2016. http://www.azquotes.com/quote/204812.

"because of early"
Attributed to Sigmund Freud.

Attitude Makes the Difference

"The longer I live"
"Charles R. Swindoll Quotes." Quotes.net. STANDS4 LLC, 2016. http://www.quotes.net/quote/17859.

Family—Raising Children

"Raising children is more"
"In an uncertain world"
Spock, Benjamin. *Dr. Spock's Baby and Child Care*, Revised Seventh Edition. Pocket Books. 1998.

"It's not who you are in life"
Godwin, Alan. E. "Infecting Your Kids with Integrity." The Ethics & Religious Liberty Commission, Aug 20, 2007. https://erlc.com/article/infecting-your-kids-with-integrity.

"You cannot impart"
Hendricks, Howard G. AZQuotes.com, Wind and Fly LTD, 2016. http://www.azquotes.com/quote/608802.

"As a parent, teaching"
Chen, Tony. "Raising Kids of Good Character: Integrity." Savvy Daddy. http://tony.sunflowerwww.net/raising-kids-strong-character-integrity.

"Abraham Lincoln Speaks"
Akinlami, Taiwo. "Abraham Lincoln Speaks: 'The Fate of Humanity is in the Hands of the Child.'" https://taiwoakinlami.wordpress.com/2013/02/02/abraham-lincoln-speaks-the-state-of-humanity-is-in-the-hands-of-the-child.

Teaching With Integrity

"Soskil Empowering Students"
Collins, Katie. "Soskil empowering students to do good in the world." The News Eagle. Jan. 2, 2015.

Excellence and Ethics

"One of the Tools"
Berg, Yehuda. "Daily Tune-up." Kabbalah Centre Dallas, November 3, 2012. https://www.facebook.com/DallasKabbalah/posts/43866109 952578.

"Academic Integrity"
Wangaard, David and Stephens, Jason. "Academic Integrity: A Critical Challenge for Schools." *Excellence and Ethics*. Winter, 2011.

"A wedding vow"
Carter, Stephen L. *Integrity*. Harper Perennial: New York. 1996.

Role Models

"It's amazing what happens"
"One of the greatest"
Ziglar, Zig. *Over the top*. Thomas Nelson: Nashville. 1997.

"Integrity is what you feel"
Fussman, Cal. "Ted Danson: What I've Learned." Esquire, Dec. 14, 2010. http://www.esquire.com/entertainment/interviews/a9105/ted-danson-interview-0111.

What Is an Integrity Commitment?

"Olympic athletes pay"
Attributed to Bruce Jenner.

Athletes Whose Commitment Means More

"I believe he was thinking"
Siegal, Alan. "God vs. the World Series: Sandy Koufax's Yom Kippur Sacrifice." *The Atlantic*. Sept. 17, 2010.

"But you still want to be known"
Jeter, Derek. BrainyQuote.com, Xplore Inc, 2016. http://www.brainyquote.com/quotes/quotes/d/derekjeter586277.html.

"New York Mets"
Lemperer, Jason "New York Mets: Why David Is the 'Wright' Choice for Captain." *The Bleacher Report*, March 21, 2013.

Integrity in Our Personal Lives—What Controls Your Life?

"Real Integrity is"
Oprah Winfrey. BrainyQuote.com, Xplore Inc, 2016. http://www.brainyquote.com/quotes/quotes/o/oprahwinfr386951.html.

"If you go looking for a friend"
Attributed to Zig Ziglar.

"With the knowledge"
Jim Herzfeld and John Hamburg. *Meet the Fockers*. Film. Directed by Jay Roach. 2004.

"You know the old adage"
Daily Devotions, December 20, 2012. https://thedwordshop.word-press.com/daily-devotions.

"Single Again"
Connor, Lucy. "Single Again—Where Did the Integrity Go?" CNN iReport, June 4, 2014. http://ireport.cnn.com/docs/DOC-1140478.

Integrity in Religion

"It's not what we profess"
Bacon, Francis. AZQuotes.com, Wind and Fly LTD, 2016. http://www.azquotes.com/quote/1310630.

"The integrity of faith"
Cloud, Henry. *Integrity, the Courage to Meet the Demands of Reality.* HarperBusiness: New York. 2009.

"Am I truthful?"
Walker, Paul L. "Integrity—Reality or Illusion?" The General Council of the Assemblies of God. http://ag.org/top/church_workers/ldrshp_gen_integrity.cfm.

"The reason for my hope"
Billy Graham. BrainyQuote.com, Xplore Inc, 2016. http://www.brainyquote.com/quotes/quotes/b/billygraha626304.html.

"Do They Profess Integrity?"
Efird, David. "Religion and Integrity." The Integrity Project. http://integrityproject.org/the-project/religion-integrity

"The Real Bond"
Bahá, Abdu'l. "The Real Bond of Integrity is Religious in Character." National Spiritual Assembly of the Bahais of the United States. http://centenary.bahai.us/talk/real-bond-integrity-religious-character.

The Integrity of Samuel

"The Integrity of Samuel"
Boa, Kenneth. "Integrity." Bible.com, October 24, 2005. https://bible.org/seriespage/6-integrity

Integrity and Ethics in Business

"There is a natural alliance"
Attributed to Jack Kemp.
Ziglar, Zig. *Over the to*p. Thomas Nelson: Nashville. 1997.

"Business Lessons from Islam"
Bamber, Dave. "Integrity and Dis-integrity: Business Responsibility Lessons from Islam." European Business Ethics Ireland, 2012. https://ebeni.wordpress.com/ebeni-conferences/conference/presentation/religious-integrity.

"Most of us were raised"
Miller, Adrian. *The Blatant Truth*. Adrian Miller. 2007

"Suppose that a reasonable"
Carter, Stephen L. *Integrity*. Harper Perennial: New York. 1996.

"Mainstream Media Fail"
Addams, Mike. "Mainstream media FAIL: Sleazebag doctors attacking Doctor Oz have histories of criminal fraud and ties to Monsanto's 'Discredit Bureau'." NaturalNews.com. http://www.naturalnews.com/049408_Doctor_Oz_Monsanto_Discredit_Bureau_mainstream_media_FAIL.html.

"Why Do Employees Steal"
Keating, Matt "Why do employees steal from their workplace?" The
Guardian: October 7, 2005. http://www.theguardian.com/money/
2005/oct/08/careers.work1.

Government

"Public confidence"
Adlai E. Stevenson. BrainyQuote.com, Xplore Inc, 2016. http://
www.brainyquote.com/quotes/quotes/a/adlaieste401632.html.

"In the American experience"
Comstock, Amy. "Maintaining Government Integrity: The
Perspective of the U.S. Office of Government Ethics." USA.gov:
2001. http://2001-2009.state.gov/p/inl/rls/rm/may/3403.htm.

"Integrity in Government"
Lloyd Weinreb, Integrity in Government, 72 Fordham L. Rev. 421
(2003). http://ir.lawnet.fordham.edu/flr/vol72/iss2/13.

What Is Your Ultimate Goal in Life?

"In the middle"
Attributed to Albert Einstein.

"Eleven Famous Successes"
Legge, Peter. "11 Famous Successes That Stemmed From Failure."
BCBusiness.ca.http://www.bcbusiness.ca/people/11-famous-successes-
that-stemmed-from-failure.

"Many of you may have heard the story"
Nelson, Sara. "Woman who was kept in coma for a month after being hit by flying frozen turkey forgives teenager for prank." The Daily Mail: November 10, 2010. http://www.dailymail.co.uk/news/article-1328389/Woman-hit-flying-turkey-forgives-teenager-threw-prank.html#ixzz3zyzPsOtw.

"Integrity of Our Food Supply"
Attributed to Tami Racaniello, www.itstimetogetfit.com.

Conclusion

"It's amazing"
Ziglar, Zig. *Over the to*p. Thomas Nelson: Nashville. 1997.

"After the cheers"
Williams, Pat. Vince Lombardi on Leadership: Life Lessons from a Five-Time NFL Championship Coach. Advantage Media Group. 2015.

About the Book

"The most influential tool"
Attributed to Zig Ziglar.

"Each of us will someday"
Attributed to William Arthur Ward.
Ziglar, Zig. *Over the to*p. Thomas Nelson: Nashville. 1997.

Be Connected

Visit Our Website

Go to www.NailOfIntegrity.com to read exclusive previews and excerpts of blogs, new books, newsletters and products.

Subscribe to our free e-newsletter and special discount offers

Interested in Booking a Speaking Engagement with Mr. Soskil www. NailofIntegrity.com/contact-us/

About the Author

Marvin Soskil, author, motivator, mentor, visionary and speaker a true entrepreneur by trade, has developed several concepts which each became flourishing businesses. As a spiritual and community-minded leader, Mr. Soskil has always displayed a sense of well-being to benefit others. The book, Integrity . . . When No One's Looking, evolved from of the creation of products to the passion for the subject matter and writing of a book. His overwhelming passion for the subject matter and sharing the message took precedence to his creative desire to sell my product. He hopes that through his message he can make an impact on society.

CPSIA information can be obtained
at www.ICGtesting.com
Printed in the USA
FSHW010459120721
83146FS